PSYCHOSOCIAL
STUDIES

Psychosocial Studies

Phyllis Caroff, DSW
Mary Gottesfeld, MSS
EDITORS

Foreword by Harold Lewis, DSW

GARDNER PRESS, INC.

New York & London

GARDNER PRESS, INC.

19 UNION SQUARE WEST

NEW YORK, NEW YORK 10003

All foreign orders except Canada and South America to:

Afterhurst Limited

Chancery House

319 City Road

London, N1, England

Library of Congress Cataloging-in-Publication Data

Psychosocial studies.

Includes index.

1. Psychiatric social work.   2. Social service.

I. Caroff, Phyllis.   II. Gottesfeld, Mary L.

HV689.P74   1986   362.2'0425   86-22806

ISBN 0-89876-100-X

Design by Sidney Solomon

PRINTED IN THE UNITED STATES OF AMERICA

Contents

To Harold Lewis
for his encouragement, support and commitment
to the advancement of clinical practice

Contributors

Edna Adelson, M.A.   Research scientist, University of Michigan, Department of Psychiatry, Child Development Project (retired)

Ruben Blanck, LL.M., M.S.   Consultant in psychotherapy, Beth Israel Medical Center; private practice

Phyllis Caroff, D.S.W.   Professor, Hunter College School of Social Work; director, Post Masters' Program in Advanced Clinical Social Work; private practice

Joyce Edward, M.S.S.W.   Faculty, Post Masters' Program in Advanced Clinical Social Work; instructor, Smith College School of Social Work; private practice

Eda Goldstein, D.S.W.   Associate professor, New York University School of Social Work; private practice

*Mary L. Gottesfeld, M.S.S.   Adjunct full professor, Hunter College School of Social Work; chair, Individual Therapy Concentration, Post Masters' Program in Advanced Clinical Social Work; private practice

Katherine A. Kendall, Ph.D.   First Lucy and Henry Moses distinguished visiting professor, Hunter College School of Social Work; former secretary general, International Association of Schools of Social Work

Harold Lewis, D.S.W.   Dean, Hunter College School of Social Work

Florence Lieberman, D.S.W.   Professor, Hunter College School of Social Work; coordinator, Part-time Program, Post Masters' Program in Advanced Clinical Social Work; private practice

James R. Montgomery, M.S.W.   Supervisor of social work, Psychiatric Outpatient Clinic, St. Luke's Hospital; faculty, Post Masters' Program in Advanced Clinical Social Work; private practice

Joseph Palombo, M.A.   Dean, Chicago Institute for Clinical Social Work; private practice

Mary E. Pharis, Ph.D.   Associate professor, School of Social Work, University of Texas at Austin; Willoughby Centennial Fellow in Child Welfare, University of Texas at Austin

Gerda Schulman, LL.D., M.S.   Associate professor, Adelphi University, School of Social Work; chair, Family Therapy Concentration, Post Masters' Program in Advanced Clinical Social Work; private practice

Jean Sanville, Ph.D.   Training analyst, Los Angeles Institute for Psychoanalytic Studies; editor, *Clinical Social Work Journal*; private practice

Lucille Spira, D.S.W.   Adjunct assistant professor, New York Univer-

sity School of Social Work; faculty, Post Masters' Program in Advanced Clinical Social Work; private practice

Francis Joseph Turner, D.S.W.   Director of social work, York University, Canada; Second Lucy and Henry Moses distinguished visiting professor, Hunter College School of Social Work

*Deceased, June 1984.

Foreword

In keeping with their profession's Code of Ethics, social work practitioners must stay current with the developments in knowledge that affect practice, and refrain from intervening with people in troubled situations who require help the worker lacks the competence to provide. The series of colloquia that generated the papers included in this volume are consistent with this ethical imperative, and true to the mission of the Post-Master's Program in Advanced Clinical Social Work

Hunter's Post-Master's Program in the School of Social Work evolved as a natural extension of the school's commitment to direct practice. Clinical education for practice in social service organizations has absorbed the major share of the school's resources throughout its 30-year history. The Casework sequence, under the leadership of Louise Hamilton, Phyllis Caroff, and Florence Vigilanti, has consistently sought to enrich the core masters curriculum in clinical work. The decision to extend the educational offering to postgraduate level at the initiative of Phyllis Caroff, with the support of Florence Lieberman of our faculty and a talented group of practitioners, represented the Schools' recognition that more advanced preparation for clinical practice was necessary, but could not be accomplished within the time frame of a master's curriculum.

The success of this Program, and the quality of the papers presented here, attest to the wisdom of those who have consistently advocated collaboration of school and field in generating new knowledge and sharing new uses of knowledge. But beyond the merit of the concept and the effort of faculty and service providers, the Program would not have succeeded without the devotion, intelligence, and hard work of Irene Schaefer and Ali Taylor, whose administrative skills made impossible tasks manageable.

Harold Lewis

Introduction

Phyllis Caroff

This collection of papers has been selected from presentations at a series of scholarly meetings sponsored by the Post Master's Program in Advanced Clinical Practice at the Hunter College School of Social Work. The first advanced clinical practice program under the auspices of a school of social work, the program is unique in that both academicians in active clinical practice and sophisticated clinical social workers able to communicate their competence in an educational arena collaborated in its design and implementation. Thus relevance of content to teaching and learning has been assured. It also reflects the commitment of its Program Policy Committee to the shared responsibility of the academic and practice sectors of the profession to provide for the continuing education of its clinical personnel.

Clinical social work is emerging from an extended period of neglect by the profession. The education and legislative activities of the National Federation of Societies of Clinical Social Workers, and the recent acceptance by the board of the National Association of Social Workers (NASW) of a "Definition of Clinical Social Work" and "Standards for the Practice of Clinical Social Work," as well as the association's clinical programming and legislative involvement, demonstrate current responsiveness to the interests of the clinical membership. It is of note that members of the Program Policy Committee have led many of the activities within both the National Federation and NASW that have helped the profession, as well as the larger community, to recognize clinical social work as an important psychosocial treatment which includes psychotherapy.

This volume would not be possible were it not for the creative impetus provided by the late Mary Gottesfield. Mary saw it as obligatory that the program contribute to the literature to advance clinical practice, its values, knowledge, and skill. That social work clinicians, who are in the forefront in the delivery of psychological and social treatment services, have failed to have

1

an impact on the larger professional community in terms of their theoretical knowledge and practical wisdom was a matter of concern to her, as it is to us who complete the work we began together.

Her selection of papers, the first of which was presented in 1978, during the first year of the program, was intended to address both the breadth and the depth of the substantive areas in which some of our most gifted clinicians have been involved—a kind of clinical bouquet. The format, a formal presentation followed by the response of a discussant, is used here, as it has been at virtually all of the meetings promoted by the program. The intent has been to demonstrate that openness to inquiry and dialogue are a sine qua non to advance our understanding and to contribute to the quality of life for our clients.

The first six presentations, with their discussant counterparts, address three broad areas. Under the rubric of social phenomena and their implications for our work with clients are "The Illusion of Sexual Equality: Progress or Regress? (Sanville and Gottesfeld) and "The Witches: Mothers in Therapy" (Lieberman and Spira). Sanville's paper was written in 1977. Now the positives and the problems of the social-sexual revolution are being reevaluated by many in our society. These chapters point up the challenge involved in maintaining our sense of direction, continuity, and balance during rapid social change.

Advances in theory development and the impact on clinical practice are represented by "Clinical Issues in Self Psychology" (Palombo and Goldstein) and "Further Extensions of Theory and Practice" (Blanck and Montgomery). These chapters substantively contribute to our theoretical practice and knowledge base, and make visible the process by which such advancement occurs.

Contributing to that still very complicated and ill-defined area called clinical research are "The Emotional Birth of the Family" (Pharis and Edward) and "Clinical Research: Encounter with Reality" (Adelson and Schulman). These two chapters are examples of the range of subject matter appropriate for a study called "clinical," the variables deemed necessary for the phenomenon called behavior to be understood and changed, and the various methodological approaches. These contributions help us to see that we are at a beginning stage in addressing the complexities of clinical research.

Two papers presented under program auspices by the School of Social Work's first and second Henry and Lucy Moses Distinguished Visiting Professors were chosen for inclusion because of their particular relevance to clinical social work (chapters 7 and 8). Thus Kendall contributes her first-hand knowledge of the highlights of the advent of American casework on the European continent, presented to the graduates of the Post Master's Program in Advanced Clinical Social Work in September 1983. Turner addresses "Ethnic Factors and Clinical Treatment," the focus of his study during his residence at the school as the second Moses professor. The paper was presented at the most recent Annual Distinguished Visitors Lecture, a tradition instituted by the program at its inception.

As noted this brief review of the volume's content has been organized according to the substantive areas that guided our selection—the impact of social phenomena, advances in theory and practice, and clinical research, with the additional two papers. The papers are presented in the chronological order of their delivery and span the period from 1977–1985. To facilitate reference use, a précis of the paper and of the related discussion precedes each chapter. Editing has been limited to those modifications which, in the editors' view, highlight the scholarship. While references to the particular meeting in which they were presented were deleted, together with personal interjections, every effort has been made to retain the personal style of the clinician at work. We deem this essential to retaining the quality of the process.

Marry Gottesfeld died in June 1984 prior to the completion of this book. This work is but one of the many contributions she made to the development of the Post Master's Clinical Program at Hunter, to which she was devoted. Her positive influence on many of the faculty and students in the individual therapy concentration and on the Program Policy Committee members was significant. Many of our authors are equally indebted to her for the stimulation and encouragement she provided in advancing their work in the profession. Working together often involved a struggle, but her knowledge, integrity and commitment to excellence in the profession made it possible for us to negotiate our differences and to regard their resolution as providing a better outcome in our work. This volume is a tangible recognition of her essential contribution to the quality of our program.

As director of the program, I speak for all of us involved in it in expressing the hope that the continued excellence of presentations under its auspices will make other such collections possible. In this way Mary Gottesfeld's dream of excellence will be continued.

1 *The Illusion of Sexual Equality: Progress or Regress?*

Jean L. Sanville

"And those calm shining suns of morn
They ask not who is maid or boy."—*Goethe; (quoted by Freud (1911, p. 29)*

The dream of equality between the sexes, how it came about, its source of power, whether it is illusion or delusion, and its importance in clinical work are examined in the context of a changing social milieu. Case examples underscore the greater struggle for women in achieving sexual equality. Those most likely to realize the universal dream will do so through efforts to increase self-awareness, and through this contribute selectively to changes in the culture.

DISCUSSION by Mary L. Gottesfeld The concept of "primary illusion," symbiosis, and the empathic perspective à la Kohut as evidenced in the author's work are considered in light of current developmental theory. The necessity to study the earliest experiences of life—to reexamine psychological theory while retaining the integrity of technique—is perceived as the important message of this chapter.

In 1911 Freud described the case of a Dr. Schroeder, who fantasied that souls, after undergoing a process of purification, enter into a *state of bliss*. Schroeder declared that male bliss was superior to that of the female, however, as it consisted of the contemplation of God, whereas female bliss was an uninterrupted feeling of voluptuousness. But as he pondered this division of delights, Schroeder became discontented and longed also for the sensual pleasures he thought reserved for the other sex. His solution was to imagine his own transformation into a woman so that he could claim both religious ecstacy and sensuous gratification. In a footnote (p. 29) Freud comments, "It would be much more in keeping with the wish-fulfillment offered by the life beyond that in it we shall at last be free from the difference between the sexes."

5

EQUALITY AND IDENTICALITY

The idea of equality and the idea of identicality seem inextricably intertwined in the human mind. We imagine that to enjoy the prerogatives of an admired or envied other, we must become that other—we must appropriate its attributes. Today both men and women are impatient to break free of former role restrictions. They are not willing to wait for the life beyond to actualize fuller potentialities, but are striving to encompass in their own beings qualities traditionally assumed to be limited to the "opposite" sex. They are not satisfied to achieve these changes through the *delusions* of paranoid thinking. Some devote themselves to a reforming of the social surroundings so that experimentation is safe; others emphasize a reforming of images of the self. It is part of the thesis of this chapter that those who are most likely to approximate a realization of the universal dream of equality employ a dialectic process that attempts to increase self-awareness from which societal changes selectively derive. Thus the realm of playful illusion is extended for themselves and others.

SOCIAL MILIEU IN TURMOIL

The reshaping of the social milieu that is evident throughout the Western world is dramatically observable in California, where I practice psychotherapy. California is the land of Synanon, whose leader persuaded members of his flock to "change partners," to divorce their old spouses and trade them in for new ones. It is the locale of Sandstone, a lavish institution in the Santa Monica Mountains dedicated to the exploration of open sexuality. One attends with a partner; both disrobe and are free to engage in sexual exchanges with other partners in full view of everyone, including the "primary" mate. It is the home of Alex Comfort, whose books on sexuality have been translated into the world's languages. One analyst colleague recently lauded those writings as having done more to free humankind from its sexual hang-ups than has all of psychoanalysis. It is the headquarters for a *professional* sexual surrogates association, with membership dependent upon completing a training course and an internship. The group sets "standards of aptitudes and attitudes," requirements for continuing education, and a code of ethics. The prestigious University of California at Los Angeles sponsored a Conference on Professional and Legal Issues in the Use of Surrogate Partners in Sex Therapy, at which featured speakers included reputable legal and mental health practitioners together with some of the surrogates themselves, one of whom is a licensed clinical social worker who publicly advertises the services of her clinic. An organization of prostitutes, COYOTE (Call Off Your Old Tired Ethics), lobbies to change the interpretation of laws that discriminate against prostitutes but go easy on their clientele. This organization maintains a clinical social worker as a consultant. And, of course, there is the film industry of Hollywood, grinding out movies that increasingly depict sex in explicit fashion, both "straight" and deviant, for both the big screen and television. Pornography is big business. Therapy, too, is fairly big business, with a plethora of offerings available, including nude marathons and all the touchy-feely approaches.

Perhaps California is like the rest of the Western world, "only more so." The new options abound: sexual experiences by adolescents; couples living together without marriage; marriage without children; children without marriage, including adoption by single men as well as single women; members of both sexes living as singles by preference; age differences in play-mating (Sanville & Shor, 1975); homosexuality and lesbianism; and the development of communes and other "alternative life-styles." Permissiveness for experimentation is unprecedented.

Clinicians can view these social phenomena, even those that seem rather mad, as they view individual symptoms—as manifestations of a desire to make something better, to overcome old obstacles to states of bliss. Although the reformers, like our patients, draw upon the energies of a basic underlying wish, their ignorance of the nature and dimensions of that wish leaves them without guides to a more inclusive repair. Thus their programs tend to tackle one problem in the relationship between the sexes as though its solution will be the total answer, and initial high hopes tend soon to be dashed. In fact some commentators on the scene declare that the attempted remedies have only exacerbated the difficulties between men and women.

In clinical practice we rarely see those who are shocked by contemporary changes, who recoil from and denounce them as the workings of the devil. Nor do we see those, less emotional perhaps, who perceive in current activities a jeopardy to values that should be cherished, such as those involving marriage and the family. But neither do we treat many at the other extreme—those who, ridden by impulse, enter into the drama in an insightless fashion, using its options to serve the stereotyped demands of their anxieties. Our patients are more likely to be people who seek help in overcoming the fears and constrictions that prevent the "owning" of bodily feelings that can be *fun*, or who have wearied of licentious behaviors and wish to overcome growing jadedness, longing to restore a spiritual quality that could reinstate sensual feeling. Most of all we are consulted by those who are trying to extricate themselves from unsatisfactory traditional relationship patterns; who want to equip themselves to gain from and to contribute to a greater equality between the sexes, which they imagine could result in greater fulfillment. They wish to be able to use the new options to undo their traditional ways of thinking and doing. In their play with those options, they are extending them, and creating and recreating the culture in which we live.

THE HAZARDS OF INEQUALITY

Writing in 1772 "Of the Pernicious Effects Which Arise From the Unnatural Distinctions Established in Society," Mary Wollstonecraft declared:

> There must be more equality established in society, or morality will never gain ground.... It is vain to expect virtue from women 'til they are in some degree independent of men; nay, it is vain to expect that strength of natural affection which would make them good wives and mothers. Whilst they are absolutely dependent on their husbands they will be cunning, mean, and selfish, and the men who can be gratified by the fawning fondness of spaniel-like affection have not much delicacy, for love is

not to be bought, in any sense of the word; its silken wings are instantly shriveled up when anything beside a return in kind is sought. . . .

Entreating men to "emancipate their companions," she promises:

Would men but generously snap our chains, and be content with rational fellowship instead of slavish obedience, they would find us more observant daughters, more affectionate sisters, more faithful wives, more reasonable mothers—in a word, better citizens. We should then love them with true affection, because we should learn to respect ourselves; and, the peace of mind of a worthy man would not be interrupted by the idle vanity of his wife, nor the babes sent to nestle in a strange bosom, having never found a home in their mother's.

It was impossible even for a liberal woman such as Mary Wollstonecraft to foresee some of the long-term effects of this striving for equality and it may be impossible for us now to foresee the consequences of what has been achieved and what will be achieved. We note with certainty, however, that women have not been willing to wait for men to emancipate them, and one of the phases in becoming freer entails disentanglement from the strictures of family life itself.

Women are becoming increasingly aware that marriage can be bad for their mental health. In my practice is a group of women in late middle age, women whose children are grown. All are feeling a terrifying stalemate in their lives; they had devoted themselves to their traditional roles, and now, most of them divorced or separated, they feel themselves empty of the resources with which to enjoy the years ahead. The only one who still lives with a husband is the most self-effacing. She has abdicated all power over the years, making a "success" of her marriage by becoming a nonperson. She has, incidentally, a recurrent sexual fantasy of being a powerful and significant woman, using men to gratify her sensuous whims, deigning to show them favors when they please her, but otherwise dismissing them in peremptory fashion. As clinicians we have developed a painful awareness of how many women have utilized marriage as a defense, out of fear of testing their wits and capabilities at the university or in the workplace. Now, in addition to the long-standing inner obstacles, they confront "real" hurdles in a world that has little use for persons unskilled and inexperienced in work outside the home. And, to make matters worse, they are suffering the stigma that the feminine liberation movement is felt to attach to being a "mere housewife."

Women are wary, too, of what Ellen Peck has termed *The Baby Trap*. A large proportion of my female adolescent patients declare their intention not to bear children. No doubt many later change their minds. But some find that, when they do, the males with whom they are involved do not want to father more babies, since they may already be supporting children by previous wives and have "had it" with parenthood. Among those women who marry young and bear children early, many find the burdens of family responsibility too great and become runaway wives—a social phenomenon now just as pervasive as that of the abandoning husband. The women whom I have seen clinically who had resorted to this "solution" had strong desires to be *more* than wives and mothers, and utilized their uneasy escape to set about becoming, if not always more, at least different from the subservient persons they felt themselves to have been.

It is not mere coincidence that at this time in history, when there is greater sexual equality than ever before, the incidence of marital dissolution is at its peak, and that the breakup of the family is leaving many children with the feeling that they have no bosom in which to nestle. And yet the profound conviction persists—that increasing autonomy of women, their equality with men, will lead to better intimacy between the sexes. What is this dream of equality? From whence does it come? From whence does it derive its power? Is it illusion or delusion? And what is its import for us as clinicians in our therapeutic work?

ORIGINS OF THE WISH FOR EQUALITY

Inequality between the sexes has a very long history. It exists among all primates, although for our purposes we should note some "cultural differences." Tree dwellers who, compared with their ground-dwelling relatives, have less need to defend themselves from predators, manifest less sexual dimorphism (i.e., the males are not appreciably larger than the females); there is less or no male dominance, a less pronounced male hierarchy, and greater sexual indiscriminancy (Gough, 1975). Thus when the scene was safer, there tended to be greater equality, not only socially, but also on a biological level. The upright position that freed the hands for tool use meant confronting greater dangers and risks.

One of the prices of the advance to the status of Homo sapiens seems to have been a cultural division of labor that, although intended for survival purposes, was destined to entail inequality between males and females. Human babies, who required large heads to hold all that capacity for language and symbolism, thus had to be born earlier, and they needed prolonged care. Their mothers assumed the roles of caretakers, while their fathers guarded the unit and hunted for food. Femaleness thus *took form* out of the actions connected with childbearing and childrearing, while maleness *took form* out of the actions of protecting and providing. The family was, along with tool use and language, one of the most important developments in the human revolution, without which civilization would have been impossible. From the start then, woman's status was tied to her role in the family, a role subordinate to that of the man. Although some historians in the liberation movement have tried to see it otherwise, there seems never to have been a glorious period when women managed to gain ascendancy. But, says Kathleen Gough (1975), "It is not necessary to believe myths of a feminist Golden Age in order to plan parity for the future" (p. 46).

What then are we to hypothesize to be the origin of the ineradicable wish for equality between the sexes and the conviction that it will lead to fuller loving? Joel Shor and the writer (1978) have posited that it begins in the psychological state of the infant at birth, a state we have called the *primary illusion.* There is, we imagine, in those first postnatal days, a dreamlike quality to existence, an "illusion of fusion," oscillating with only an evanescent sense of self and of other. It would be a state free of conflict, there being no perceived difference between the baby's wishes and desires and those of the mother. There would be no need for power, as coercion is unnecessary when all one's wants are gratified, and the needs and wishes of the other are identical to one's own. There is just the flowing feeling of comfortable union alternating with a sense of completeness in one's own being, an "illusion of self-sufficiency."

Of course, there is the inevitable fall from paradise. Even with the good-enough mother, there are occasions when the baby will be deprived of important supplies, suppressed in its functioning, and, in time, frustrated in exchanges with significant others. In coping with these unavoidable pains, the infant builds up a store of defenses, which, over the years, crystalize into what we call *character*. The child adjusts to "reality," but sustains a "split of the ego." This situation, we maintain, is not altogether pathological, for via this split the individual preserves the image of perfection, while adapting to the exigencies of daily life. Those who have experienced abundantly the goodness of the initial caretaker tend to have a keener awareness of the ideal and a greater amount of energy to pursue it.

It is our assumption that this model, imprinted upon the neurological system of the infant, is the basis of the drive that persists throughout life to reinstate, in some measure, the experience of that original bliss. It is thus the psychosocial analog to the image of physical well-being that evokes processes of bodily repair. The image of the primary illusion powers the drive for repair of self, of relationships, and of the social order. Like all ideal goals, it is beyond absolute attainment, but our glimpses of its ecstasy renew our intent to reach for equality—not only between the sexes, but among all human beings. Since every inequality entails envies and tensions that preclude fresh experiences of carefree togetherness, it will also provoke us to take measures to remedy matters.

We use the word *illusion* in its original sense of "in play," and in the way indicated by Freud (1927) when he said that "we call a belief an illusion when a wish fulfillment is a prominent factor in its motivation, and in doing so we disregard its relation to reality." The dictionary definition of illusion is a "false mental image or conception which may be a misinterpretation of a real experience or may be something imagined (Random House), but the definition also states that it may be "pleasing, harmless, or even useful." "Illusion" carries a sense of irony or mockery, both of which, as we shall see, are applicable to the drama of relationship between the sexes.

It is through play that the primary illusion is preserved. As Winnicott (1971) says, "Play is neither a matter of inner psychic reality nor a matter of external reality." It is neither inside nor outside. But it involves *doing*. It is exciting precisely because of the precariousness of the interplay between personal psychic reality and the reactions of others or that which is "objectively" perceived. For purposes of repair, playing must be spontaneous and not compliant or acquiescent. It requires "safe space." This safe space is psychological space, the prototype of which is the feeling of safety of the playing child near the protective mother, and a later version of which is the playing patient in the environment created by a therapist whose central role is to promote that patient's capacities to measure for him or herself what to play, when, and for how long, and with whom and to what ends.

Play is a special way of violating fixity, and thus lends itself to the aims of those who would modify the old hierarchical relationship between the sexes. There are always risks involved, of hurt to oneself or to others. The skill of any given player and the experience in and consequences of the action will depend upon the degree of ego strength that has been attained: the ability to make finely attuned judgments about the resources and dangers from within as they are matched or mismatched by the opportunities and jeopardies from without, and to modify one's behavior in accordance with these estimates. Persons who have sufficiently developed such capacities may be in a position to utilize the permissiveness of today's society to arrive at greater autonomy for themselves and at more satisfactory patterns of togetherness.

Women in particular are seen engaging in behaviors that might once have been labeled "acting out," but when looked at nonjudgmentally, their actions may be found not to be "driven," but "ego syntonic." In appearance there is a mockery of the actions of traditional males whose ways they imitate and even caricature, but the purpose may be a serious attempt to arrive at that felt equality they sense as the necessary prelude to mutuality.

FEMALE ADOLESCENTS AND
THE NEW CULTURAL OPTIONS

Some writers have regarded the current scene as a source of danger to the psychic life and personal security of the female adolescent. Florence Lieberman (1973), for example, in her article on "Sex and the Adolescent Girl," offers abundant illustrations of the circumstances, inner and outer, under which that can be so. The ideal liberated choice, she proposes, would be that the girl "wait to develop the social, intellectual, and psychological strengths that will enable her to engage in sexual activities with security and pleasure." She views as an "unemotional" approach to sex the experimentation with intercourse of a 17-year-old "for the simple reason that she did not wish to be a virgin." When the caseworker inquired what was wrong with being a virgin, the young woman responded. "What is so good about being a virgin?" If the patient had been a 17-year-old male, would a male therapist have similarly challenged him? In any event it is important to take the young woman's retort seriously, and, attending closely to clinical data, ask whether some females may now indeed be furthering their liberation by awarding themselves the right to experiment with sexuality prior to "real relationships," and even with promiscuity, a prerogative once reserved for, and perhaps even encouraged in, male adolescents.

In 1892 Krafft-Ebing wrote of the tendency of women to fall into "sexual thralldom," and Freud further developed this theme in his *The Taboo of Virginity* (1918). What both were describing was that the woman whose desire for love has been held in check for so long tends to take the first man who gratifies her into a close and lasting relationship, and to be henceforth unavailable to any other. There is a kind of "sexual imprinting," with the woman manifesting a high degree of dependence on the man who took her virginity. But although Freud saw this one-sided binding as "indispensable in maintaining civilized marriage," he was also aware that because of the paradoxical nature of the woman's reaction to defloration—

pleasure, but also anger and the impulse to revile the "first man"—a degree of "archaic enmity" became a component of the relationship. Indeed, said Freud, that is why some first marriages are poor and second marriages turn out better!

Today we might extend Freud's explanatory principles. An additional source of the woman's wrath may have been her sense of foreclosure, the narrowing of options and choices, the abandonment of hopes for autonomy, the continuing dependence on this man for basic supplies, both physical and emotional. She must, on some (unfortunately inarticulate) level of her being, have sensed the risk, and her own lack of insurance to cover it—the vulnerability of abandoning one's self without the confidence that one could safely reclaim it if necessary. In other words she entered into a fusion without first claiming her ability to stand alone, to be independent. When the first intercourse symbolizes such dangers, it is inevitable that hostility ensues.

In primitive societies in which people did not separate psychical from physical dangers, some vague risk was apprehended when virginity was "taken," which was guarded against by having someone other than the bridegroom deflower the bride. Clinical data on the psychological consequence of what might appear to us to be ritual rape are not available, but we might hypothesize that today's young women might *choose* defloration by someone about whom they do not particularly care precisely to avoid sexual thralldom. It could be part of the process of creating a self able to choose a mate on some basis other than sheer physical attraction, a self without the hostilities that could spoil a love relationship. Such a choice would be of particular interest to those who are rather consciously concerned with breaking out of traditional patterns and ways.

Among my patients are young women who utilize a phase of what we might once have termed "sexual delinquency" to learn about and to remake themselves in relation to the male world. They engage in what Shor (1972) has called "self-traumatization," a successful masochistic acting out. Its purpose is repair, both of object relations and of self, and in this instance, it is specifically directed toward equalization.

Zelda, Play Acting Toward Equality

One such patient was Zelda, who first came for brief therapy at the age of 16 when she had tried to help a suicidal boyfriend. She was the middle of three children, with a pathologically obese older sister and a younger brother whom she saw as so superior that she became anxiously self-conscious just when trying to converse with him. She complained that her father, an affluent businessman, doted on her for her beauty and "feminine charms," but seemed oblivious to her mind and spirit. Her mother played the role her husband wanted of her, making herself attractive and a gracious homemaker but neglecting her intellect and other capabilities. Zelda's father termed his wife a "sexy saint." In her relationship with her disconsolate young friend, Zelda was reversing the order she perceived at home: the male caring for a helpless and hopeless female.

Zelda came for further therapy when she was 20, this time because of a feeling of guilt that she had hurt a man with whom she had had her most rewarding relationship. She described, very thoughtfully, her rampant promiscuity while in college, behavior which did not prevent her from being a top student. She slept with so many men that she could not even recall the number. In time the activity palled, as "no relationship was different from any other." She decided that she was using "freedom" to avoid possible closeness and resolved "not to fuck another man." But, just as she was pondering exploration of her "lesbian side" in the hope of finding "something in common other than intercourse," along came George. Unlike all the other men whose eagerness to take her to bed she had come to despise, George talked to her, and seemed seriously interested in learning about the women's liberation movement. They had many long and significant discussions about this topic before they slept together. This sexual experience was unlike anything she had ever had before. And although she had "not intended to fall in love," that was what happened. She was now living with George. They had made a pact of honesty, so that when either was attracted to another person, they had discussed it, and had remained faithful to each other. But then, while George was out of town on a business trip, Zelda had an affair. She was not interested in the man in other than a physical way, for he had none of George's intelligence or values, and she knew that he wanted nothing from her but a sexual encounter.

The incident was not a thrilling experience, and her love for George was unaffected by it. But, in keeping with their promise of openness, she told him about her escapade. He, to her dismay, reacted with shock and anger, declaring that she had "raped" him and that she must choose between breaking off with him or continuing with him knowing that he would never trust her again. Zelda had once been raped, so the metaphor had profound meaning for her: rape could be of the spirit as well as the body. Nevertheless she was not ready to guarantee that she would be monogamous. Although now dubious that a purely physical relationship would be rewarding, she had to feel that the choice would remain hers. Perhaps that was "selfishness," but she was, as she said, "only 20" and did not want to make premature closures.

Zelda, like many other women today, may feel the need to experiment with behaviors once reserved for, and even prescribed for, men. One of the steps toward "equality" may be to act as men have traditionally acted, to discover what such behaviors can and cannot do for them, and the likely consequences of such relationships. At least it is improbable that women will be deluded into imagining that sexual pleasure is identical to love, and when they can be conscious of what they are attempting in their experimentation, they are unlikely to fall into the role of victims. Certainly they will not be the "sexual saints" their mothers tried to be.

Whether such behaviors in any given patient are *acting out*—that is, unconscious repetition of conflict, a sort of experimental recollection—or *action* that contains attempts at conscious solutions of conflict situations will depend upon the degree of impulse mastery and ego development (Ekstein & Friedman, 1957). One could characterize Zelda's promiscuity and infidelity as *play acting* (which is somewhere between the two), a preconscious trial solution with a fair degree of "secondary process domination," or attempts to prepare for the future by role taking. In her identification with males by imitating them, she begins to establish her own autonomy. When these experimenting young women are in treatment, the most useful response of the therapist will be to interpret the underlying reparative wish, that is, the wish for the feeling of equality that could make mutuality possible. Once equipped with this understanding, there is little danger that the actor will be driven to continue living out the part in actuality. The wish will become conscious intent, and the woman will be in a better position to weigh the instrumental value of action to achieve that intent.

Thanatos is essential to the process of change, to the breaking up of old patterns to make way for the new. It is perhaps inevitable that the women's liberation movement should manifest in its ranks so much hostility and enmity toward men and that so many of the women's efforts at repair should take the form of doing unto others what they feel was done unto them. But we might guess that, just as with individual patients, they will discover the limits of such means to attain that which they want for themselves—the autonomy that will permit them fuller illusions of equality and of fusion.

ILLUSION AND LOVE

It has long been recognized that there is an equivalence between loving and being loved, but many authors have distinguished between masculine and feminine versions of love. Jekels and Bergler (1952), for example, declared that in feminine love the woman looks up to the object, stands in subjection to it, demands and enjoys the object's care, and demands emphatically to be loved in return. In masculine love, on the other hand, the concern is with patronizing, benevolent ruling, and caring for and spending upon, with the return of affection less important. Both project the ego ideal onto the object and partly reintroject it, with the consequent raising of self-esteem, sometimes to a level startling in its similarity to the "exalted mood of the manic." But the male, they write, "arrogates" the attributes of the ego ideal, whereas the female experiences the *illusion* of satisfying the ego ideal by being loved by he who personifies it. Thus, in their opinion, love is a consequence of the feeling of guilt.

In translating the concepts described, it could be said that, traditionally, neither men nor women have been able to attain full adult versions of primary love. The male too has his *illusion*—that of self-sufficiency. (Jekels and Bergler hid it in the word "arrogate," which means to claim unwarrantably or presumptuously.) Since the female's illusion is of fusion, lacking equal possibility of oscillating to the stance of self-sufficiency, she remains closer in position to the child, in whom those authors saw anxiety as the motive for love. It may be easier for her to feel "I am nothing, the partner is everything" and "I become everything by being permitted to participate in the partner's greatness." As Fenichel (1945) said, the passive aim of female sexuality is more closely related to the original aims of incorporation than is the active aim of male sexuality. Male patients today often ask for help in transcending some dimly perceived hurdle to fulfillment in love. They want *passion*, which, we should remind ourselves, in its etymological roots is the opposite of *action*.

William, Questing for Mutuality

William, who was in his late 50s, came to treatment complaining of an inability to love the woman with whom he was living. He found her beautiful to look at and imagined the envy of other men when he exhibited her at Hollywood gatherings. But he saw her as unintelligent, uneducated, uninterested in the activities he would like to pursue, and unable to discuss the ideas in which he was interested. He had dreams in which he cast her into the role of a maid who spoke in a foreign tongue, and who, to his embarrassment, sat down with his guests at the table. He prided himself on his tenderness toward her, as evidenced by her often telling him, "You are so good to me." But he frequently became frustrated with her limitations and lost his temper, which made him feel guilty. In describing their intercourse, he used the language of the streets. He wanted to "fuck her in the rear," but she wouldn't let him. The "strong orgasm" of which he sometimes boasted contained destructiveness along with its erotic aim; he gained physical release but not a spiritual experience. He was openly angry and disappointed in her because she never "came" with him. But it was not only in bed that they did not "come together." It was not possible for William to project his "ego ideal" onto this partner, because his image of her was that she was all he deemed bad: helpless, dependent, succumbing to inertia and stagnation, limited in her interests, chronically irritable. With her as the repository of these qualities, he could safely disown them, and feel superior. He "arrogated" power, independence, ambition, and energy, as well as wide-ranging involvement, initiative, and tolerance. Of course, he could not experience that "feeling of flowing together, of losing one's individuality, of achieving a desired reunion of the ego with something larger which has been outside" of the boundaries, that "identification on a higher level" that is the "height of full genital satisfaction" (Fenichel, 1945), since that which was "outside," the woman in his life, could not possibly be imagined as "larger" than he.

His *identification* was with her as "part object"; that is, he could empathize with her helplessness, which evoked memories of childhood traumas of his own. There were so few things that they both enjoyed that they were not acquiring that store of conjoint memories that can arise from *participation* in activities in which they engaged together. Both of these rendered their *communication* sparse and constricted, and they were not traveling the pathways to mutuality that Shor and Sanville propose in *Illusion in Loving* (1978). Yet their pattern of inequality was not appreciably different from that of the traditional relationship between men and women: he out in the world gaining satisfaction from his instrumental role while surreptitiously gratifying her need for dependency by her cooking and taking care of his clothes, and she, confining herself to house and home, experiencing some envy of his position but fearful of reaching out for a fuller life for herself.

With William, however, the one different feature is that he, after some years of analysis with a male therapist, now sought a woman with whom to work on his felt problem—the inability to experience strong amorous feelings or desire. Using the transference as a playground (Freud, 1914), he provoked himself to permit that idealization characteristic of those in love and to confront the anxieties that were stirred up by assuming such a regressive stance. It was difficult for him to "take things in" from me; for a long while he exhibited a sort of psychic deafness whenever I spoke. The idea of *equality* was foreign to him. If he saw me as intelligent and independent, he became apprehensive that I might be more intelligent, more self-reliant, than he. How terrifying that a woman might be stronger than a man! She could even contemplate leaving her man, as he contemplated leaving his woman, for she would not *need* him. He handled that terror by engaging in fantasies of raping me, subjugating me by sexual prowess, and thus got in touch with his own use of sexuality to handle his fears by imagining conquering and possession.

FROM REPARATIVE WISH TO REPARATIVE INTENT

The stance of the therapist throughout such cases involves not just pointing up the defenses, but constant interpretation of the *reparative* wish contained even in those maneuvers of the patient that are self-defeating. The emphasis is on the yearning to attain the felt equality that would render unnecessary the exercise of *power* on the part of either man or woman, and that could then lead to more experiences of new versions of the primary illusion. With this purpose clear, patients are enabled to look at the obstacles, inner and outer, and to work for the progression that could permit benign regression (Balint, 1959). Thus may the reparative wish be converted into a *reparative intent.*

Clinically we often observe that females, like Zelda's mother and William's lover, are more ready to reexperience the aspect of primary bliss that is the *illusion of fusion,* and that males, like Zelda's father and William, tend to aim at the aspect that is the *illusion of self-sufficiency.* Thus neither males nor females reared in traditional culture find it easy to recreate a full version of the original paradise—an easy oscillation between the two aspects, a dialectic that keeps both relationships and the sense of self ever evolving.

MYSTERY AND LOVE

At least one critic of *Illusion in Loving* has accused its authors (Joel Shor and I) of engaging in mysticism because we would highlight the unconscious *purpose* behind human behaviors. I no longer recoil from that accusation, but have come to see it as absolutely appropriate that we should freely acknowledge our "belief in the existence of realities beyond perceptual or intellectual apprehension but central to being and directly accessible by intuition" (*American Heritage Dictionary*). We agree with Kenneth Burke (1945) that a kind of grammatical repression has been at work as we have been taught not to use teleological terms, but that *purpose* may nonetheless "surreptitiously survive" (p. 291). As clinicians we are concerned with intuition, and like Burke, would view intuition as "not a mere passive perception, a datum of sensory [or even supersensory] *knowledge*. It is an *acting-with* . . . a wider orbit of meanings," the mystery centering in an *image* (in this instance, that of the primary illusion), which stands for an inarticulate *act* or *idea* (the idea of equality and of mutuality, of being and doing together, but without permanent loss of individuality). The word intuition comes from the Latin *intueri*, meaning to look at or toward, to contemplate. If indeed intuition has been "God's gift to the feminine woman," these feminine women have propounded to give it also to their men, and their men want to receive it. It is the *purpose* of much of the push toward equality that the sexes want to extend their capacities to know each other intuitively.

Robert Stoller (1974) has declared that mystery is "so important to sexual excitement that the two are almost synonymous." Pondering why sexual perversions are more frequent and more "fiercely bizarre" in men than in women, he posits that in our society male children are, even more than female chidren, prohibited from *looking* to find out about anatomical differences between the sexes, and how dangerous they may be. Along with those of us trying to rethink psychoanalytic concepts about sexual development, he sees the boy as having special difficulties because his body is unlike that of the mother, with whom he first identified. The male is left with rage at having to give up that early bliss, with fear of not succeeding in escaping from the identification, and with a wish for revenge because the mother put him into such a predicament. Like Dr. Schroeder, he tries to end the mystery by creating perverse acts or fantasies that deny differences or that stress his superior equipment—that is, by demonstrating that the difference is without threat. He becomes fixated on these "solutions" through the experience of physical pleasure that accompanies the satisfaction of revenge, and through his feeling that he has taken and surmounted the risk; they become "unalterable by life experience or treatment."

Stoller suggests a return to analytic study for clues to how aggression (activity) is converted into hostility (Stoller, 1974). I would add that we should also seek clues to how hostility and violence may be converted into aggression (activity). While Stoller explicitly describes hostility and mystery in perversions, he also sees hostility as essential to all sexual "turn-on." So, if we diminish the hostility between the sexes by fuller identification, expanded participation, and richer communication, will we not thereby diminish the joy in sex? Will the illusion of equality abolish mystery? Or may it not be that there will persist a "truer kind of mystery, now hidden behind the fog of social inequality?" (Burke, 1969b).

The word *mystery* is related to the greek *müein*, which means "to shut the eyes," but also to *müein*, which means "to initiate into the mysteries." Thus it hints at the dialectic, as *mystery* describes both the *passive* reflection of class (or gender) culture, and an *active* way of maintaining cultural (or gender) uniqueness. Men and women may want to open their eyes to each other and to merge in illusory fusions, but they also want to be free to create new mysteries in illusory separateness, so that the play of social evolution can go on.

REFERENCES

Balint, M. 1959. Progression for the sake of regression. In *Thrills and regressions*. New York: International University Press.

Burke, K. 1969. *A grammar of motives*. Berkeley and Los Angeles: University of California Press. (Originally published by Prentice-Hall, Englewood Cliffs, N.J., 1945.)

―――. *A rhetoric of motives*. Berkeley and Los Angeles: University of California Press. (Originally published by Prentice-Hall, Englewood Cliffs, N.J., 1950.)

Ekstein, R., and S. Friedman. 1956. The function of acting out, play action and play acting in psychotherapeutic process. *J. Am. Psychoanal. Assoc.* 5.(4):581–629.

Fenichel, O. 1945. *The psychoanalytic theory of neurosis*. New York: W. W. Norton, p. 85.

Freud, S. 1911. Psychoanalytic notes on an autobiographical account of a case of paranoia. *Standard edition*, vol. XII. London: Hogarth Press, 1958.

―――. 1914. Remembering, repeating and working through. *Standard edition,* vol. XII. London: Hogarth Press, 1958.

―――. 1918. The taboo of virginity: Contributions to the psychology of love. *Standard edition*, vol. XI. London: Hogarth Press, 1958.

―――. 1927. The future of an illusion. *Standard edition*, vol. XXI. London: Hogarth Press, 1958.

Gough, K. 1975. The origin of the family. In *Women: A feminist perspective*, J. Freeman (ed.). Palo Alto, Calif. Mayfield, pp. 43–63.

Jekels, L., and E. Bergler. 1952. Transference in love. In *Selected papers*, L. Jekels (Ed.). New York: International Universities Press.

Lieberman, F. 1973. Sex and the adolescent girl: Liberation or exploitation. *Clin. Soc. Work J.* 1(4): 224–243.

Perk, E. 1976. *The baby trap*. New York: Pinnacle Books (paperback).

Sanville, J., and J. Shor. 1975. Age games in play-mating. *Clin. Soc. Work J.* 3(3).

Shor, J. 1972. Two principles of reparative regression: Self-traumatization and self-provocation. *Psychoanal. Rev.* LIX (2).

―――― and J. Sanville. 1978. *Illusion in loving*. New York: International Universities Press. Penguin paperback, 1979.

Stoller, R. J. 1974. Hostility and mystery in perversion. *Int. J. Psycho-Anal.* 55:425–434.

Winnicott, D. W. 1971. *Playing and reality*. New York: Basic Books.

Wollstonecraft, M. 1772. Of the pernicious effects which arise from the unnatural distinctions established in society. In *Countertradition*, S. Delany, (Ed.). New York: Basic Books, 1971.

DISCUSSION

Mary L. Gottesfeld

I first read of Jean Sanville's work on changing role values of men and women in her 1973 paper with Joel Shor, "Leading

Ladies and Gentle Men." Like the present presentation, this first paper had that quality of thought, grace, and literate charm so typical of their work on this subject, which culminated in their book *Illusions in Loving*.

My comments are in two parts. The first part addresses specific theoretical and technical implications of her thesis, and the second part, its broader implications.

For me the core of the chapter is that the search for equality between the sexes is based on a wish to regain the earliest state of pleasurable fusion with the mother, the state called the "primary illusion." Sexual equality is not then "progress" as much as it is "regress" to an earlier state, and to attain this without a loss of individuality would lead to both equality and mutuality in relationships. Further, the drive for this perfect state persists throughout life and is the force behind reparative urges in ourselves, our relationships, and the social order. It may never be attained, but it serves a benign purpose in provoking us to reach for social and personal equality.

Contemporary analysts are promulgating a new view of the early bond between mother and infant. One of the major contributors to this has been Margaret Mahler, who has made clinical observations of children and whose seminal work on separation and individuation is well known. I would have to assume that the state of the "primary illusion" described by Sanville is similar to what Mahler calls the symbiotic stage. Mahler postulates that at birth the infant is in an essentially objectless state, which she calls "autistic." In about the second month, this gives way to symbiosis where the infant is in a state of mutuality with the mother, and this sense of dual unity is remembered and longed for in different degrees throughout life.

I do not get a sense that Sanville is suggesting the kind of structural developmental view we ascribe to Mahler and to Otto Kernberg, but rather she seems to be describing more of an empathic state, which would lead me to believe that she may be more in sympathy with the views of Heinz Kohut. Kohut proposes an empathic perspective in understanding the patient via his accounts of his own experience, as opposed to the structural developmental viewpoint inferred from observations of the mother–child relationship.

In the case of Zelda, Sanville does not, of course, address the symptom of Zelda's promiscuity, but chooses to understand it empathetically as a reparative wish to achieve again early feelings of equality.

I make these comments about the relationship I perceive between the idea of the primary illusion, the symbiotic stage, and the empathic perspective not to confuse matters, but to show the relationships to current developmental theory. It is at this point that I would like to enlarge the scope of my comments and say why I believe that this kind of work eventually will contribute to an overall theory of psychotherapy.

Sigmund Freud did not begin to develop ego psychology until rather late in his life. Therefore, his major formulations on the development of personality—male and female—emphasize sexual development and little emphasis is placed on the inclusion of ego factors. Clearly ego psychology is strongly influenced by cultural awareness and much less by instincts. Present-day ego psychology has far less of a culture-bound quality than earlier Freudian thought. I point this out in partial explanation of why the search for sexual equality, which seems to be more a feminine search than a masculine one, has come to us so late. It is only in the recent past that society has allowed those women who did not find traditional roles appealing the opportunity to consider options regarding marriage, maternity, and employment. Some of those aspects of our cultural revolution that have given impetus to the search for sexual equality were colorfully described by Sanville in her opening description of the "California scene."

Where do the illusion of sexual equality and the theoretical notion of the primary illusion take us? They take us into the realm of rethinking some of the psychological tenets that have been so dear to us. If women such as Zelda are engaging in casual, exploratory sex in ways formerly permitted only to men, then our male/female role values are not what they used to be. To gain this new kind of personal freedom, women (and men) must also face the confusion and discomfort that come from having less structure to their lives. Furthermore, as Sanville notes, sexual freedom has also meant an increase in marital dissolutions. Therefore, the family as we know it, with a strong father and a nurturing mother, no longer exists; it has been replaced by a much more egalitarian parental model. It means, further, that children today must relate to stepmothers and stepfathers, half-siblings, stepsiblings, and adopted siblings, as well as full siblings, and, in some instances, to a single parent or many parents. The days of the clear Oedipus complex and the development of the superego may be numbered—at the very least, they are changing. Even our thoughts about gender identity have changed considerably, as we no longer view it—as Freud did—as starting with the oedipal phase, but with the very early life of the child, and the powerful effects on the child of parental attitudes.

It is no wonder that with the diminished strength of the oedipal family we see fewer patients with symptoms. At the same time, we see an increasing number of patients with existential complaints, and so we must study in greater depth the earliest of life's experiences, the psychological birth of the infant and even, as we have learned from Jean Sanville, the primary illusion. This readiness to explore the earliest frontiers of psychological knowledge and to reexamine psychoanalytic theory while not—as we learned from her case material—sacrificing the integrity of analytic technique, is the significance of this chapter.

2 *The Emotional Birth of the Family*

Mary E. Pharis

The first pregnancy as a discrete stage is the focus of this chapter. It underscores the significance of parental development for the healthful psychosocial context into which the infant will be born. Based on the assumption that expectant parents build "conglomerates of images and ideas" regarding the meaning of the pregnancy to their own lives, the concept of parental models was developed. Data from two of four completed studies are presented. The author's conception is supported by the differences found between the parental models of the two groups. The delineation of the features of an optimal first pregnancy provides a potential assessment guide with inherent opportunities for preventative intervention.

DISCUSSION by Joyce Edward The discussant questions the conclusion that differences between comparison groups are wholly a function of a favorable developmental outcome of the first pregnancy. It is necessary also to assess the developmental features achieved during marriage or a sustained relationship as well as the impact of the lack thereof in prepregnancy. It is noted that parental models and expectations about life when a child is born have their origins in early childhood experiences and become modified through preceding developmental stages in addition to the special form during the first pregnancy. There is concern about the underattention to unconscious models of the mind and their potential to undermine conscious expectations of parents in their role. Also, the increasing reliance on intellectual and technical knowledge must be evaluated in light of experiences that may depend "more upon feeling than knowing."

Social workers are keenly aware that, in the United States, opportunities to intervene on behalf of children and families in difficulty are limited in the child's early years.

Until a child enters school at the age of five, there are built into our social services delivery system very few entry points into the family system for either assessment or intervention. Child abuse complaints, major accidents or illnesses of child or parents, and cases where the child shows early serious developmental delay are among the few instances in which social services personnel may gain access to the family before the child enters school, except in cases where the family is formed by adoption.*

In one day, in New York City alone, some 300 women give birth (*Vital Statistics of New York State*, 1977); they are among the 3.25 million who will give birth this year in our country. Yet few of those 300 babies, or of the 3.25 million babies, will come to our attention any time soon. Thus, relatively few out of our population of nearly 15.5 million children under the age of five, and relatively few of their families, have ever been screened or evaluated by professionals interested in family functioning from a broad perspective. Yet in all likelihood our best hope for influencing family functioning in beneficial ways comes in those early years.

From the premise that the first pregnancy is a discrete stage in adult development, with particular characteristics and distinctive features, it would appear to be the ideal time for professionals to *evaluate* the nature and status of the family even as it is in formation. It is also an ideal time to *influence* the process of formation.

BACKGROUND OF FAMILY CONTEXT STUDY

By way of justifying a set of specific recommendations for assessment, and out of the belief that first pregnancy is a discrete developmental stage, the following presents the background of a program of research on the variations in the parental context into which babies are born. Details of that study, as well as conclusions about the aspects of preparation and expectation that

---

*Families receiving public assistance are not included, as social work contacts with such families do not provide legitimate opportunity for entry into the family system for evaluation or assessment of any sort.

particularly merit our attention in evaluating expectant parents, are included.

Many researchers hope that if we can identify developmental deviations of all sorts at an extremely early age, we will be more successful in intervention. Infancy research is booming in the United States and elsewhere (Haith & Campos, 1977).

Psychologists, nurses, pediatricians, and other child development specialists observe and record parent–infant gaze interactions, vocal exchanges, holding styles, "reciprocity," activity patterns—literally every breath and heartbeat—in incredibly minute detail during the first days of the baby's life, and even in the delivery room (Mcfarlane, 1977: Stern, 1977).

The general public shares this rising interest in infancy. Clarke-Stewart (1978) documents the amazing rate at which our society now consumes books and articles about infancy and child care. She estimates that over 4.5 million books are purchased annually by readers interested in infant and child development. Noteworthy also is the astounding growth of popular interest in such issues as methods of delivery, modes of feeding, and types of hospital care. The LaLeche League, the advocates of LaMaze and Leboyer deliveries, and the emphasis on "bonding," which in turn has led to the dramatic increase in "rooming-in" arrangements, all testify to increased interest in infancy on the part of both the general public and professionals.

But despite this interest and the research activity regarding the topic of infancy and parent–infant interaction, there has been little systematic study of the psychosocial aspects of the *context into which a baby is born.* In the terminology of systems theory, there is much more study and interest in the *components* of the system (the parent and infant), and the *dynamics* of the system (the interaction, or reciprocity, or patterns of behavior exchange) than in the *environment* of the system.

The writer has argued elsewhere that the family is born in the mind of expectant parents long before the baby actually arrives (Pharis, 1977). Psychologically and emotionally the family is born before the baby is born. It is important for professionals to understand the parental concept of infants and family *as an index to the psychosocial context that exists before the birth of the baby.*

We know that the 300 new mothers whose babies are born in New York on a given day will be going home to various surroundings, or contexts, in the next few days. They will carry their infants home with different expectations, to different social circumstances. Some things are already known about context. We know "in our bones" that to be poor and pregnant is not promising; to be ill and pregnant is not promising; to be unwed and pregnant is not promising. But we know much less about the emotional and psychological aspects of the prenatal context. Some parents will greet their new baby with greater joy and eagerness, and with a greater sense of personal readiness for parenthood, than will others. We do not know what exactly it is that makes for such differences.

The question may be asked: "Is there any support for the notion that differences in psychosocial context, as revealed by differences in prenatal expectations and attitudes, for example, may be crucial?" One might answer that we have nothing to lose by studying the family as it forms during pregnancy, since most research to date with newborns and their parents just has not achieved the sought-after goal of enabling us to predict how the family will do later. The baby's own postnatal behaviors and the parents' behaviors do not correlate at all well with their functioning at later time periods (Kagan, 1980).

One prominent researcher in psychology, Arnold Sameroff (1980), has begun to argue that this may be true because the major continuities in development are more associated with *the contextual differences in which development occurs*, such as racial differences, socioeconomic status (SES) differences, and cultural differences, than in specifics of the individual behavior of either parent or child. He would say that if we hope to predict anything at all about a child's development, it may be more important to know the race and SES level of that child's parents than the amount of time the mother spent with the infant on its first day of life, the temperament of the infant, or the score the child obtains on the Bayley Scales of Infant Development (1969) at six months of age.

Various research studies give Sameroff's argument support. Betty Caldwell and her colleagues have developed a research instrument (Bradley & Caldwell, 1976; Elardo et al., 1975) called the Home Observation for Measurement of the Environment (HOME). This device taps the environment of a home in six specific areas. Variables assessed include the kinds of playthings available to a child, the number of books, the daily routines in the home, the organization of the physical space, and such specifics of parent–child interaction as the number of times per week that the father eats dinner with the family. The HOME inventory successfully discriminates between samples of various educational and economic backgrounds. In one sense it gives an operational definition to the SES contextual differences to which Sameroff calls attention. Therefore, consider this interesting finding. If the family context is evaluated with the HOME inventory when the child is six months old, and the child is also tested with the Bayley Scales of Infant Development, and then at age three the child is given the Stanford-Binet IQ test, it is found that the HOME scores correlate with intelligence at age three better than the child's own earlier score on the infant development scale.

Another study, by Willerman and co-workers (1970), has also suggested that SES may act as a powerful moderator variable where the child's intellectual development is concerned. Out of over 3000 white infants in the famous collaborative study who had been tested with the Bayley scales at the age of eight months, these researchers identified a subgroup of infants who had scored very poorly on the early developmental test, in the lowest quartile. These children had also been tested with the Stanford-Binet test when they were four years old, and Willerman and colleagues reevaluated the data to determine if there were any effects related to the family's social class.

For the children from lower SES homes, a poor score on the Bayley at eight months was associated with a poor score on the Stanford-Binet at four years. But for children from higher SES homes, a child's poor score on the Bayley at eight months did not carry the same dire prognosis: at age four, children in higher SES homes who had scored poorly at eight months scored slightly above average on the Stanford-Binet.

Despite such clear indications that some aspects of the environmental situation into which a baby is born may have a powerful impact on development, there has been surprisingly little study of those pertinent aspects of the prenatal ecological environment (Bronfenbrenner, 1979) that might identify differences in environmental context in a manner similar to Caldwell's.

STUDIES OF PARENTAL MODELS

At the University of Texas at Austin, we have developed a research program around the thesis that in order to grasp the real meaning of the various parent–infant interactions that child developmental researchers are now charting, and to determine what is indeed typical and atypical, we will need to understand more fully the variations in the parental context that exist prior to the baby's birth.

Our effort to understand the psychosocial context into which children are born led us to develop the concept of parental models. As an important aspect of parental adaptation during pregnancy, we assumed that expectant parents were building models, or conglomerates of images and ideas, regarding the meaning of the pregnancy in relation to their own lives. The concept of parental models was seen as manifesting at least three distinct aspects: models of the infant, models of the parenting role, and models of how life changes following the birth of a baby.

Each of these aspects was in turn assumed to be complex and multifaceted in nature. That is, a parent's model of the infant might include a model of a normative infant, its abilities at birth, its pace of development, the degree of difficulty it might have with various bodily functions, and the like. At the same time, a parent might entertain a model of a "good" and a "bad" infant; in addition, as a distinct subcategory of the parent's model of the infant, there might exist a fantasy model of what the parent's own coming baby actually will be like.

In a similar fashion, the model of the parenting role might include expectations and attitudes as to what the average parent is like, and what a "good" and "bad" parent might be like. Moreover, the model of parenting held by any particular expectant mother or father might well include some estimate of what he or she will actually be like in that role.

Likewise, the model of how life changes following the birth of a baby might include ideas about the number of areas in one's life that change as a result of becoming a parent, as well as the degree to which those changes are seen as major or minimal; in addition, parents might hold a model of how life changes that reflects expectations for changes in either a positive or negative direction.

Individuals' parental models were expected to reveal themselves not only through direct statements of expectations for infants and the parenting role, but also via the timing and type of concrete preparations for a baby, such as selection of names, preparations of living space, purchases, reading, and the like. Parents' reports of such subjective responses as dreaming, and daily thoughts of the coming infant, pleasure with the pregnancy, and confidence in regard to specific child-care tasks, were also seen as appropriate for inclusion in an evaluation of the psychosocial aspects of preparation for a baby.

Our hope is that the concept of parental models, as one means for operationalizing particular aspects of the environmental and emotional contexts that exist prior to a baby's birth, will provide a versatile and useful set of "descriptors" of psychosocial adaptation in pregnancy.

To date we have completed four studies of parental models. The first was a pilot project with 25 couples expecting a first child. In this study we recorded and analyzed parents' responses to a series of broad and open-ended questions designed to inform us of the areas of interest: the information they had about infants, and their concerns, and fantasies, and the concrete preparations they had undertaken for the coming babies. Out of the answers we received, we constructed a format for more formal study of parental models. In our second study, we compared the parental models of 20 younger couples expecting a first child with those of 20 older couples who were also expecting a first child. In our third study, we evaluated the parental models of 25 male and 25 female undergraduates who were not married and were not parents. And in our most recent study, we looked at some aspects of parental models among 125 single, high-school students. Thus parental models as they are influenced by age, sex, and pregnancy status have been assessed (Baenen et al., 1979; Pharis, 1978; Pharis & Manosevitz, 1980).

The studies are too lengthy and complex for all the findings to be reviewed here. But because they are especially informative about *the nature of first pregnancy among low-risk parents*, some findings that pertain to differences between the 80 expectant parents in study 2 and the 50 unmarried students in study 3 are briefly reported. Table 2-1 shows the relevant demographic characteristics of these 80 expectant parents and 50 students.

We found that almost all of the college students who participated in the research had already decided that they wished to have children some day. Students reported wanting families with a slightly higher number of children: 2.56 children was the mean reported by students, whereas the expectant couples were planning on families with a mean of 2.06 children.

Moreover, both students and expectant parents had previous contacts with infants that were equivalent. All reported in detail on their prior contacts with infants during three time periods in their lives, and out of 36 relevant items, a scale was created to quantify previous child care. Although women in all groups reported significantly more prior child care, there was no significant difference between students and expectant parents in previous contact with infants.

Despite equivalent prior contact with infants, however, and despite an apparently positive orientation toward babies and parenthood, findings indicated that the students and the expectant parents had consistently different parental models. Nowhere was this clearer than in their expectations for the life changes parents will experience following a baby's birth.

Students and parents were asked 35 specific questions regarding changes that might occur in the year following a baby's birth; Figure 2-1 shows a subset of the "change" items. Various analyses indicated that the patterns of responses between the two groups were entirely different in three ways. First, students expected that more of the 35 items would change; they circled "no change" on a mean of only 12 items, whereas expectant parents thought a mean of 16 items would not change at all in the first year after a baby's birth. Second, students expected the changes would be more extreme, they more often circled +3's or -3's. Third, students expected that changes would be in a more negative direction; they more often reported they thought the good things would decrease and the bad things

Table 2-1

Characteristics of Samples in Parental-Models Research Studies

	Age	Days Pregnant	Education to Present, Years	Years Married	SES Level
Pilot study: 50 expectant parents					
25 females	25	252	14	4	III
25 males	27		15		III
Study 2: 80 expectant parents					
Younger couples					
20 females	22	235	14	2	III
20 males	24		14		III
Older couples					
20 females	31	238	16	6	III
20 males	32		17		III
Study 3: 50 single college students:					
25 females	19	—	13		II
25 males	20		13		II
Study 4: 123 single high-school students:					
62 females	16	—	10	—	III
61 males	16		10	—	III

Notes: All subjects were white with the exception of one mother in the pilot study, who was Japanese. All expectant parents were married. No subject had previously been a parent. SES classification based on Hollingshead's occupational index applied to occupation of subject's father.

IN THE FIRST YEAR AFTER THE BABY IS BORN

−3 = Very much less than before
−2 = Somewhat less than before
−1 = A bit less than before
0 = No change from before
+1 = A bit more than before
+2 = Somewhat more than before
+3 = Very much more than before

	Less (Decrease)			No Change			More (Increase)
	−3	−2	−1	0	+1	+2	+3
cc. Will the amount of food you will eat each day increase or decrease?	−3	−2	−1	0	+1	+2	+3
dd. Will the amount of alcoholic beverages you will consume increase or decrease?	−3	−2	−1	0	+1	+2	+3
ee. Will the number of fights you will have with spouse increase or decrease?	−3	−2	−1	0	+1	+2	+3
ff. Will you feel more physically attractive than before or less attractive?	−3	−2	−1	0	+1	+2	+3
gg. Will you feel more clear about who you are and where you are going in life, or less clear?	−3	−2	−1	0	+1	+2	+3
hh. Will the amount of money you will be able to put in savings increase or decrease?	−3	−2	−1	0	+1	+2	+3
ii. Will the amount of satisfaction you feel in the sexual relationship with your spouse increase or decrease?	−3	−2	−1	0	+1	+2	+3

Figure 2.1 Sample change items.

would increase. And when we looked at the specific items, it was clear that students more often saw the birth of a baby as intruding more on social activities, thus leading to less leisure time, more worry and decreased feelings of attractiveness.

With respect to beliefs regarding the abilities babies have in the first weeks of life, students and expectant parents again differed. Out of 18 specific items, some of which are shown in Figure 2-2, students believed that babies had fewer abilities at birth. On another set of items we asked everyone to rate the degree of difficulty they believed babies have in the first weeks with such functions as eating, sleeping, and spitting up. These items, originally developed by Broussard (1964), are shown in Figure 2-3. Students rated babies as having more difficulties than did expectant parents. Students also rated themselves as having less confidence that they could perform 12 specific child-care tasks such as feeding, diapering, and bathing, despite the fact that they had reported equivalent practice with such items on the scale of prior child-care contacts.

All participants were asked to give estimates of the age at which babies typically achieve certain developmental milestones, such as when they first sleep through the night, roll over, sit up, stack three blocks, take a first step. On 14 such items from the Bayley Scales of Infant Development (1969), students gave estimates that indicated they believed babies develop at a much slower pace than was estimated by expectant parents.

Thus, as compared with expectant parents, students were less confident that they could handle specific child-care tasks; they viewed babies as having more difficulties and fewer abilities at birth; they expected babies' development to progress at a slower pace; and they thought babies changed a parent's life more and in a more negative direction. These, and other, differences existed despite the fact that students had equivalent previous child-care contacts, and a positive orientation toward becoming parents themselves in the future! Incidently, a series of additional analyses of the data convinced us that the differences reported here are not a function of age differences between students and expectant parents, but are related to the fact that the one group was pregnant whereas the other was not.

NEWBORN INFANT ABILITIES AND ACTIVITIES . . .

Please fill out the following list, circling your answers. Consider a "newborn baby" to be an average child that is in the FIRST WEEK OF LIFE.

a. Can a newborn see a toy held up in front of it?	Yes	No	Don't know
b. Can a newborn hear loud sounds like a door slamming?	Yes	No	Don't know
c. Can a newborn hear soft sounds like quiet talk in the next room?	Yes	No	Don't know
d. Can the newborn see in color?	Yes	No	Don't know
e. Can the newborn smell odors?	Yes	No	Don't know
f. Can the newborn taste different flavors?	Yes	No	Don't know
g. Can the newborn feel heat?	Yes	No	Don't know
h. Can the newborn feel cold?	Yes	No	Don't know
i. Can the newborn feel pain on the skin?	Yes	No	Don't know
j. Can the newborn feel inside, like stomach pain?	Yes	No	Don't know
k. Can the newborn look where it wants to, voluntarily?	Yes	No	Don't know
l. Can the newborn turn its head where it wants to?	Yes	No	Don't know
m. Can the newborn suck by itself without learning?	Yes	No	Don't know
n. Can the newborn grasp objects in its hand?	Yes	No	Don't know
o. If the newborn is holding something, can it let go voluntarily?	Yes	No	Don't know

Figure 2.2   Sample abilities items.

For the following items, enter in column at right the following appropriate code:

1 = None
2 = Very little
3 = Moderate amount
4 = A good bit
5 = A great deal

a. How much crying do you think the average baby does?

b. How much trouble do you think the average baby has in feeding?

c. How much spitting up and vomiting do you think the average baby does?

d. How much difficulty do you think the average baby has in sleeping?

e. How much difficulty do you think the average baby has with bowel movement?

f. How much trouble do you think the average baby has in settling down to a predictable pattern of eating and sleeping; a schedule?

g. How fragile do you think the average baby is; that is, how much care do you think has to be taken in handling the average baby?

Figure 2.3 Sample difficulty rating items.

SOME CHARACTERISTICS OF AN
OPTIMAL FIRST PREGNANCY

On the basis of these differences between the parental models of students and expectant parents, then, we have concluded that a first pregnancy may be considered a discrete developmental stage that features marked changes in complex patterns of belief and behavior. The nature of the particular changes that define first pregnancy as a developmental stage provides a means for inferring the characteristics of an optimal first pregnancy. As shown in Figure 2-4, this study of optimal or low-risk individuals in a first pregnancy found that pregnancy and parenthood were accompanied by (1) increasing clarity about infants and the parental role; (2) increasingly positive evaluation of a newborn infant's abilities; (3) increasingly earlier expectations for the pace of an infant's development; (4) increasing confidence in one's own ability as a caretaker; (5) decreasing anxiety about parenthood as a whole; (6) decreasing estimations of the amount of difficulty babies have in the first weeks of life; (7) an increasingly positive view of how babies affect parents' lives, with lowered expectation of negative changes and lowered estimation of the degree to which babies intrude on parents' activities.

The implications for assessment and intervention by social workers and other service professionals are enormous. To parents in a low-risk population, a baby looked as if it would be

---

1. An increased sense of clarity about babies and the parental role.
2. A greater expectation that babies are born with a number of sensory, perceptual, and motor abilities.
3. Expectations for earlier infant development.
4. Increased confidence in their own parenting abilities.
5. Lower anxiety about parenthood in general.
6. Lower expectations for the amount of difficulty babies have in the first weeks of life.
7. A more positive view of how babies affect parents' lives.

Figure 2.4 Characteristic parental expectations in an optimal first pregnancy.

more fun, more able and responsive, less disruptive, and less difficult to care for; and parenthood was viewed with less anxiety and more confidence. Pregnancy for these couples was a period of rising expectations and increasing optimism, as well as dramatic change.

The dramatic nature of the changes associated with this stage of adult development suggests that first pregnancy would be an ideal time to provide services to young couples. Expectant couples are typically very eager to share the experience, and thus receptivity to such services is enhanced. We do not believe, as do some researchers, that "crisis" is an appropriate label for the nature of the experiences in a first pregnancy, but prefer the term transition as a more appropriate description. But crisis intervention theory notes that *any* period of marked internal and external upheaval increases our opportunities for providing useful intervention, and we would agree that first pregnancy offers that potential.

We think also that our parental-models approach provides a useful framework and some principles that social workers and other professionals may utilize to evaluate any individual expecting a first child. In particular, we think professionals should seek to understand the expectant parent's psychosocial status in three areas: the individual's view of himself or herself in the parental role; the expectations for infants in general, and the coming baby in particular; and the expectations that the expectant parent has for how the baby will change the parent's life. We can evaluate these three areas to determine if the optimal process, outlined by our research, is occurring.

EVALUATION OF THE CONTEXT OF A PREGNANCY

To translate these models into specifics for evaluating individuals or couples, such an evaluation would ideally be conducted at three time periods: at some point in the pregnancy, perhaps the third trimester; at the time of delivery, and on day one or two; and again in the early months after the baby has been born.

During the prenatal period, the assessment of the general economic and social circumstances of the expectant parents is important, as it is when individuals apply for services in our agencies. The stability of the parental relationship and the social situation will be prime considerations.

In addition, it will be significant to know how the parents view themselves in the parenting role. Their prior contacts with infants and their confidence in their abilities as caretakers are relevant to their view of themselves in this regard. Also to be evaluated are the parents' specific preparations for the coming baby. What kind of thinking and reading have they been doing, and what concerns might they have? What kind of concrete preparations do the parents want to make, and when do they begin? To what extent are these preparations a shared activity?

The model of infancy should inform us about their expectations for their early interactions with their baby. What abilities do they think the baby will have at birth, and what early difficulties? How have they been getting along with their baby so far—that is, has the pregnancy been an easy or a difficult one, or have there been complications?

The developing image they have of their own infant can be explored. Do they have an idea of its gender? In our studies we find that expectant parents will not state any *preferences* for the gender of the coming baby, but 78 percent of them have a sufficiently strong idea about its gender that they will chance a prediction. Do they think their baby is more active in utero than "the average baby?" Often they do, despite the fact that in a first pregnancy they can have no real idea of what activity level is "average."

This last question introduces an interesting element that has been useful and important in our studies to date. Such a question calls for comparing one's own coming baby with "an average baby." In our studies we ask participants to make many such comparisons. The idea for such a comparison was originally Broussard's (Broussard, 1964; Broussard & Hartner, 1971). Broussard and Hartner determined in a ten-year follow-up study (1976) that when mothers do not see their own infant as better than average within 72 hours of birth, the likelihood that the infant will encounter developmental difficulties increases greatly. Clearly such questions call upon intrapsychic processes in parents that are extremely important to the child's development. It seems probable that it is not only natural but also crucial for psychologically healthy expectant parents to view their own baby as special and better than average. We have been calling this phenomenon, which is very robust in our studies with low-risk expectant parents, "progenocentrism." Its existence in the prenatal period constitutes a precursor to healthy parental attachment.

In addition to looking at the models of the infant and the parenting role that any given expectant parent may hold, the degree to which the individual expects the baby's birth to alter his or her life can be evaluated. All other things being equal, an individual in a first pregnancy who anticipates that the baby will intrude a great deal, will alter a large number of personal and social habits, and will generate changes for the worse in life-style is an individual who is at greater risk than one who expects to integrate the baby smoothly into the pattern of life that exists in the home.

At the time of delivery, professionals can again use a parental-models framework to assess the degree to which the parents' expectations have been met, or not met, by the actual events of labor and delivery, and the actual baby. I believe that it would be extremely useful if professionals were available to all newly delivered mothers to discuss with them the experience of labor and delivery. Many mothers are now coming to term with very idealistic expectations for their own performance—a model of themselves as "earth mothers." The movement toward natural childbirth, and preparation courses offered by Lamaze and similar groups, often bolster these expectations. Yet many mothers find that they are unable to live up to their own expectations for themselves. Due to an astounding increase in the use of fetal-heart-rate monitors, many more mothers are undergoing unexpected cesarean sections than in the past. In one Austin hospital, cesareans account for 25 percent of all deliveries, and in another, nearly one third of all deliveries are cesareans. My impression is that for most mothers, certainly for the mother who hoped to deliver without medication, this constitutes an enormous disruption of her expectations and leads her to a sharp sense of failure just at the moment when she needs to feel a sense of accomplishment. In such situations it is essential for some profession to accept the responsibility for providing support and reassurance even beyond the time of hospital discharge.

So, too, at delivery a professional could assess the degree to which the parents' model of the infant has been met. Any deviation from normal limits in the baby's condition or in its early postpartum behavior, as defined by either physician *or parents*, should be viewed as a basis for early intervention. If nature builds in a process whereby in the optimal situation parents' expectations are rising, and the actual events cut short this process in any way, then the family is at risk at the very point at which it has been forming.

Similarly, if we argue that an optimal pregnancy is characterized by growing faith in an infant's abilities, growing confidence in one's own ability as caretaker, lowered expectations that the baby will disrupt the parents' lives, and lowered overall anxiety, then the focus for evaluation in the early months after the baby's birth is clear. The search will be for evidence that the parent is satisfied with the infant's progress, and is sufficiently well pleased with the child's abilities and characteristics, as well as his or her own ability to care for it. Here high-risk family configurations would be those where the parent identifies the baby as having more difficulty with physiological function than the parent had expected, or where the pace of the infant's development is defined by the parent as slower than expected, *even if it is in fact within normal limits.*

Parents whose confidence does not appear to be increasing over the early months, or whose anxieties about parenthood are not abating, are also likely to be at greater risk. Parents who comment about the great number of changes in their lives since the baby's birth, especially if they did not anticipate such changes or if they identify the changes as disruptive, are also parents who may be in need of early supportive and interpretive services.

CONCLUSIONS

In summary, on the basis of research with a group of low-risk expectant parents as compared with a group of students expected to constitute a low-risk population of expectant parents in the future, a picture of an optimal first pregnancy and of the context in which the emotional birth of the family occurs has been developed. The characteristics of this optimal first pregnancy have been used to derive specific suggestions for the evaluation of the context of the first pregnancy, and to identify situations that suggest increased risk.

What is it we can *do* for expectant couples, to help them prepare the most healthy context possible into which to bring their newborn?

Pointing the way to an answer to this crucial question is the evidence that our parental models are in fact intimately tied to the parents' fuller intrapsychic processes. Since parental models are forming, and reforming, in an active, intense, rich internal process during pregnancy, the fears and fantasies of expectant parents are themselves powerful in the psychosocial context.

In his wonderful *Where the Wild Things Are*,* Maurice Sendak (1963) presents a beautiful and insightful metaphoric prescription for what we must do whenever intrapsychic processes are the key.

In this classic, Max is sent to his room without supper by his mother because of a series of transgressions. There he wrestles with his most primitive impulses by going to where his "wild things" are. By going to where they live, deep within himself, he conquers the wild things and becomes their king "by the magic trick of staring into all their yellow eyes without blinking once." Having mastered his wild things by fearlessly facing them, Max returns to the world on friendly terms with his wild inner self, and more ready to find the best reality has to offer. To promote the development of a healthy emotional context in expectant parents, then, we need to help them do what Max did.

---

*Personal Note

My first acquaintance with *Where the Wild Things Are* was in Selma Fraiberg's project reception area when she was director of the Child Development Project at the Children's Psychiatric Hospital, University of Michigan. As I waited for our interview, I saw that there were many adult reading materials. This was the only children's book.

We need to help them go where their wild things are: their wild fears and primitively grandiose fantasies, their own angers, and their fierce pride in what they are creating. When we can help expectant parents to look into all the yellow eyes of their own parental models without blinking once, they, too, will become masters of the wild forces within themselves. And then they will be ready. Then they can announce the emotional birth of their family.

REFERENCES

Baenen, N., M. Pharis and C. Logue. 1979. Perceptions of parenthood and infant development: A comparison of the views of high school students, college students, and expectant parents. Presented to the American Educational Research Association, San Francisco, April 1979.

Bayley, N. 1969. *Bayley scales of infant development, manual.* New York: Psychological Corporation.

Bradley, R., and B. Caldwell. 1976. Early home environment and changes in mental test performance in children from 3 to 36 months. *Dev. Psychol.* 12: 93–97.

Bronfenbrenner, U. 1979. *The ecology of human development.* Cambridge, Mass.: Harvard University Press.

Broussard, E. R. 1964. *A study to dtermine the effectiveness of television as a medium for counseling groups of primiparous women during the immediate postpartum.* Unpublished doctoral dissertation, University of Pittsburgh.

——, and M. S. S. Hartner. 1971. Further considerations regarding maternal perception of the first born. In *Exceptional infant, Vol 2*, J. Hellmuth (Ed.). New York: Brunner/Mazel.

—— and ——. 1976. Neonatal prediction and outcome at 10–11 years. *Child Psychiatry Hum. Dev.* 7:85–93.

Clarke-Stewart, A. K. 1978. Popular primers for parents. *American Psychologist.* pp. 359–369.

Elardo, T., R. Bradley, and B. Caldwell. 1975. The relation of infants' home environments to mental test performance from six to thirty-six months: A longitudinal analysis. *Child Dev.* 46:71–76.

Haith, M. and J. Campos. 1977. Human infancy. *Ann. Rev. Psychol.* Palo Alto: Annual Review, Inc.

Kagan, J. 1980. Perspectives on continuity. In *Constancy and change in human development*, O. Brim, Jr., and J. Kagan (Eds.). Cambridge, Mass: Harvard University Press.

Macfarlane, A. 1977. *The psychology of childbirth.* Cambridge, Mass: Harvard University Press.

New York State Department of Health. 1977. *Vital statistics of New York State.*

Pharis, M. E. 1978. *Age and sex differences in expectations for infants and the parenting role among couples in a first pregnancy and among college students.* Unpublished doctoral dissertation, University of Texas at Austin.

———. 1977. The birth of the family: It happens *before* the birth of the baby. Paper presented to the Texas State NASW Convention, San Antonio.

——— and M. Manosevitz. 1980. Parental models: A means for evaluating different prenatal contexts. In *Exceptional infant IV: Psychosocial risks in infant-environment transactions*, D. B. Sawin, R. C. Hawkins, II, L. O. Walker, and J. H. Penticuff (Eds.). New York: Brunner/Mazel.

Sameroff, A. 1980. Issues in early reproductive and caretaking risk: Review and current status. In *Exceptional infant IV: Psychosocial risks in infant-environment transactions,* D. Sawin, R. Hawkins, II, L. Walker, and J. Penticuff (Eds.). New York: Brunner/Mazel.

Sendak, Maurice. 1963. *Where the wild things are.* New York: Harper & Row.

Stern, D. 1977. *The first relationship.* Cambridge, Mass: Harvard University Press.

Willerman, L., S. H. Broman, and M. F. Fiedler. 1970. Infant development, preschool IQ, and social class. *Child Dev.* 41:69–77.

DISCUSSION

Joyce Edward

This chapter makes an informative, stimulating, and felicitous contribution to our ever-increasing appreciation of the critical import of prenatal experiences for the development of parents as well as their offspring. Pharis has focused on the significance of parental development during the first pregnancy for the formation of a healthful psychosocial context into which the infant will be born, a context that will, as we know, significantly influence the well-being and development of the infant and the family. By focusing on the first pregnancy as a discrete stage in adult development, Pharis has added a dimension to Dr. Ruth Benedek's concept of parenthood as a developmental stage.

The delineation of distinct features of the first pregnancy that appear to bode well for the family-to-be provides an assessment guide that may also serve to alert the helping professional to signs of potential danger among some expectant parents. The fact that opportunities for intervention at this momentous transitional point in the life cycle exist is especially promising, as noted by Pharis. This is of deep interest to a profession that has traditionally sought to extend its capacities for preventative intervention.

Two points in this thought-provoking presentation have raised questions, though not necessarily disagreement, for me.

First, is it completely accurate to conclude that the differences in attitudes and expectations between unmarried students and expectant parents are wholly the result of a favorable developmental outcome of the first pregnancy? After all, is not marriage a developmental phase? Might it not be important to assess what developmental features are ordinarily achieved, or at least initiated, during marriage or during a sustained, intimate relationship between parents-to-be before conception, achievements that pave the way through pregnancy? It seems to me that there are such features, and it is important to assess them in relation to the expectations of those parents-to-be who have missed the opportunities for the development of their relationship associated with the prepregnancy period. This may enhance our understanding of the particular needs of those young couples who conceive immediately upon marriage, or indeed, as is the case with some of my young patients, on their first date.

Second, although Pharis asserts that the family is born in the mind of expectant parents long before the baby actually arrives, she focuses on the development of models and images regarding pregnancy, parenthood, the infant, and the family itself during the first pregnancy. I focus on what I believe Pharis would agree with, the fact that ordinarily the birth of the family in the mind begins very early. The mental models that a mother and father develop with regard to themselves as parents and their expected children, as well as their expectations of what life will be like when they are three instead of two, have their origins in early childhood experiences, real and fantasied, and become added to and modified throughout childhood, adolescence, and young adulthood. Undoubtedly they are given special shape during the first pregnancy. Our maternal or paternal ego ideals are significantly influenced by the kind of parenting we ourselves have experienced and by the kinds of inner representations we have of ourselves as children.

One of the concerns I have with the focus on the expectant parents' conscious expectations of themselves as parents is that this conscious expectation may poorly reflect the unconscious models in their minds. We are all familiar with troubled individuals who have sincerely sought to offer their offspring a healthier psychosocial context than they themselves were born into, and thus to provide themselves with a means of reparation. Such parents may repeat in their child-care practices the same traumatizing approaches and attitudes they consciously sought to avoid. The repercussions can be painful for themselves and their children. Selma Fraiberg and colleagues (1975), in an article on abusing parents, noted that while some abusing parents, raised in an abusive situation themselves, can identify with their infants in a way that permits them to treat them more empathically than they had been treated, other mothers and fathers, despite their conscious wish to do otherwise, unconsciously identify with their own abusing parents. They are driven to a repetition of their own tragic past, with themselves the aggressors and their children the representations of their own, perceived as bad, childhood selves.

Of less serious consequence perhaps is that our images of ourselves as parents are effected by the media. Our consumption of books and articles about infants and child care may attest, as Pharis suggests, to a significant and positive interest in infancy, but it also attests to an increasing reliance on intellectual knowledge and technical know-how in relation to matters that depend more upon feeling than knowing. This unfortunate reliance on books and printed guidelines is a reflection of the degree to which young parents lack adequate support systems, and in some cases an inner sense of self, that would enable them to experience a reasonable amount of confidence in their capacity to assume the tasks at hand. In view of the ever-changing patterns of child rearing, the fortunate child has been the one whose parents read the books, derived what they felt to be appropriate for them and their particular infant, and then drew from their own developmental experience and inner sense of self to guide them in their attunement to their child. Some of us remember when a generation of mothers was advised by the experts to follow rigid feeding schedules and to avoid touching their offpsring any more than was absolutely necessary. Fortunately the great majority of mothers picked up their babies and fed them in accord with their particular needs, though often guiltily. It is probably safe to hypothesize that relatively few of those infants ended up on analytic couches 20 to 30 years later.

I think, too, that there is a danger that excessive reliance on the literature may contribute to an unrealistic picture of parenting as well as of one's own personality and marital relationship. Overidealized expectations may well lead to disappointment and loss of self-esteem, and in some parents to depression. Pharis has illuminated this point well in her consideration of the painful consequences for some couples who are unable to follow through on their expectations for themselves in regard to natural childbirth. Perhaps the greatest danger is to those parents who are intrapsychically poorly equipped for parenthood and who are most likely to seek help from the so-called textbooks on infant care. What they derive in this way, if it is their primary resource, may enable them to respond to questions raised in such studies in a way that masks potential danger signals that more openended questions might reveal.

I would like to elaborate on two of the features Pharis has noted as indicators of favorable development during the first pregnancy. The first is not one that Pharis distinguishes as a favorable indicator, but it is a feature that I see as positive. I was struck by the fact that in the minds of the parents questioned, there already appears to be some degree of differentiation in the mental representations of parents and infants in what was termed the wished-for self-images and wished-for images of the infant. Incidentally the questionnaire stimulates a degree of differentiation insofar as it specifically inquires about expectations concerning the infant and expectations concerning the parents. In passing I have wondered if the completion of the questionnaire may not in itself be a helpful intervention for some parents, to the degree that the answers elicited encourage the capacity to appreciate that the baby-to-be is from the beginning a unique individual as well as a member of a family in formation. Out of the work of Margaret Mahler, Rene Spitz, and others we have come to see how essential it is for a parent to possess the capacity to engage initially in a symbiotic relationship with the developing neonate and yet at the same time to be sensitive to the infant as a separate entity. Healthy neonatal development during the symbiosis, which paves the way for healthful separation and individuation, requires attunement, not merger, on the part of the mother, though from the side of the child it is experienced as if they were one. The mother creates the symbiotic orbit by way of tuning into her infant's particular needs; this requires, for example, an ability to feed the infant when it shows signs of hunger, not when the mother feels hungry. I do not know whether the Pharis questionnaire can alert us to those troubled mothers who long for an infant to be a part of themselves and who regard and treat the neonate as a part of their own being, creating a kind of parasitic symbiosis that leads to profound problems in the developing child.

Finally, I comment on Pharis' assertion that it is crucial for a favorable developmental outcome that expectant parents view their own baby as special and better than average. This reminds me of the contributions to developmental theory of Lichenstein, Kohut, Mahler, and others. Kohut speaks of the importance of the "gleam in the mother's eye," which, I think, in part conveys the importance to the developing infant of the positive mirroring of the admiring parent who sees the infant as special. Increasingly we are becoming cognizant of the enormous significance of the affirmative, responding actions of parents in the earliest days and months of life. Lichenstein has suggested that the very sense that "I am" requires an affirmation by those who tend the infant early in life. In the absence of this affirmation, such children fail to achieve an emotional conviction of the reality of their own existence. Though they may not become psychotic, they are likely to develop to be adults who, though they display adequate ego competencies, manifest a sense of emptiness, a sense of lifelessness of painful proportions. If we can identify during pregnancy the absence of this obligatory expectation illusion of one's child's specialness and above-average potentialities, then our next challenge is to discover helpful interventive strategies. Freud has stated that "that which the fond parent projects ahead of him as his ideal in the child is merely a substitute for the lost narcissism of childhood." I suspect that among those parents who do not develop favorable expectations of their coming offspring are those individuals who concern clinicians so much today, those persons who suffer from disorders of the self. I would suggest that perhaps one of the modest interventive strategies that might be helpful is precisely what Pharis is doing. Through our attention to parents-to-be, whether through studies, services, or other means, we are affirming their particular specialness.

REFERENCES (DISCUSSION)

Fraiberg, S., E. Adelson, and V. Shapiro. 1975. Infant-mother relationships. *J. Am. Acad. Child Psychiatry*, 14:378–421.

3 Clinical Issues in Self Psychology

Joseph Palombo

Major contributions of the psychology of the self are summarized, highlighting its congeniality and applicability to the practice of clinical social work. Clinical issues that affect practice are considered. The focus, however, is on the curative dimensions of the approach, with rich clinical examples providing the illustrations for discussion of the theory's major tenets.

DISCUSSION by Eda Goldstein Based on some of the fundamental differences between self psychology and Kernberg's integration of ego psychology with object relations theory regarding the treatment of narcissistic pathology, Goldstein questions empathic introspection as a primary tool of diagnosis and treatment, omitting the systematic understanding of the patient's developmental level. Given the powerful transference and countertransference phenomena characteristic of work with this client group, a descriptive and developmental diagnosis are required as a safeguard for both patient and therapist, she contends.

As clinicians we have always been curious about the nature of our interventive tools. What is curative about our therapeutic efforts? What is it that we do with people that is helpful? We perceive ourselves as agents for change whether we adhere to the problem-solving approach (Perlman, 1970), the psychosocial approach (Hollis, 1970), the functional approach (Smalley, 1970), or the behavioral approach (Thomas, 1970). Although social work theorists have paid considerable attention to the variety of interventions, little agreement exists as to the specific manner in which the intervention helps the client or patient.

In the 1969 symposium in honor of Charlotte Towle, seven theories of social casework were presented, each by the leading exponent of that position. In her summation Bernece Simon (1970) noted:

All treatment approaches have a goal of change, modification, or improvement in relation to the situations that come to the attention of the caseworker. Within the global goal, however, there are differences in the extent of change envisioned; in the focus for change and in the definition of change. . .it may be that basic differences among the theories are found in the idea of change. The idea of change itself may be the heart of the difficulties in the formulation of treatment theory. (p. 375)

It is also to be noted that the approaches to treatment in social casework have been influenced by a heritage of derived theory. Each major position owes a large debt to another discipline from which theoretical constructs have been borrowed, and which have been woven into its fabric. Whatever the sources of the assumptions, there flows from them a logical set of propositions, which at a minimum spell out the following: a view of human nature (a psychology), a theory of the causes for dysfunctional development, and a prescriptive set of interventive propositions (practice principles) which, if implemented, would produce the desired change. The issue of change is focal only to the prescriptive propositions, as they contain a particular value system that reflect a societal set of norms to which we are committed.

THEORETICAL FRAMEWORK OF SELF PSYCHOLOGY

Psychoanalytic theory has been a fountainhead from which many social work theorists have drawn. Yet it is neither unitary nor impermeable to change. Freud's monumental work has provided a foundation upon which many have built their own superstructures. Self psychology began as an offshoot of psychoanalytic theory, and has developed into a framework that complements that theory. The contributions of Heinz Kohut (Kohut, 1971, 1977; Ornstein, 1978) have begun to be acknowledged outside psychoanalytic circles. But perhaps in no other profession have these contributions been as welcome as in clinical social work. The comfortable compatibility between the clinical principles of self psychology and clinical social work is now being accorded the recognition it deserves (Palombo, 1976).

The historical unfolding of Kohut's psychology of the self has been traced to major problems in ego psychology and psychoanalytic clinical theory. On the one hand, the tripartite model of the mind is best suited to explaining oedipal phenomena and neurotic problems, and less well suited to the understanding of preoedipal disturbances. On the other hand, empathy accepted as an important tool for therapeutic intervention had never been consistently used and systematically applied. Its primacy in matters dealing with human psychology had not been clearly conceptualized.

For a large group of patients, the clinical theory that evolves from ego psychology was not adequate for providing prescriptions for treatment. These were the people who once were identified as having "character disorders," and who are now frequently referred to as borderline or narcissistic personality disorders. The interventive approaches of insight through interpretation of repressed conflict and of ego support were ineffectual with this type of patient; at times they provided temporary relief but produced little permanent change.

Furthermore, empathy had always been considered an essential ingredient in all helping effort and had been seen more as a quality brought to the helping process by the therapist than as a systematic tool to be used systematically for the observation of a patient's intrapsychic state. Ego psychology had led to inconsistent applications of the empathic stance. It made the therapist a viewer of a patient's intrapsychic state, but it also placed the therapist in the role of an adversary to the patient's resistances. The perspective, in shifting from external to internal to the patient, led to problems in relating to the patient's direct experience of his or her affective states. Rather than acting as benign observer of the patient's internal struggles, the therapist alternated between the intrapsychic and the psychosocial perspectives.

Another way of describing this is that structural theory "is oriented to subjective experience with respect to adaptation to an objective environment" (London, 1980, p. 340) whereas self psychology is oriented to subjective experience as reflective of inner cohesion and continuity within the context of a tension between ambitions and ideals and skill and talents.

The psychology of the self attempts to remedy both flaws in the theory: the metapsychological and the clinical-theoretical. This chapter summarizes some of the major contributions the psychology of the self can make to clinical social work, with special attention to the clinical issues that affect our practice. The focus is on the curative dimensions of this approach.

Within this framework psychoanalytic psychotherapy is envisioned not simply as a modification of psychoanalysis, but rather as a subdiscipline of social casework. It is one of several modalities clinicians use in working with people. The parentage claimed for this content, is, therefore, dual: social casework and psychoanalytic psychotherapy.

THE EMPATHIC INTROSPECTIVE POINT OF VIEW

In his 1959 paper, Kohut proposed that in psychological matters tools for observation and data collection are essentially different from those used in physical sciences. In the physical sciences, use is made of the perceptual senses to measure, record, and observe events; in contacts with human beings, these tools are inadequate to give data about states of mind. Only through a different order of observation do we come to know about another person's internal psychological state. Vicarious introspection involves a merger with the patient that leads the therapist to experience what the patient is experiencing. Through self-observation and introspecting upon what is happening within him or herself, the therapist may infer the patient's feeling states. This complex process, which involves a merger while maintaining a degree of separateness, and while cognitively observing one's internal state, we call empathic introspection. Here the focus is not on what may be observed externally, nor is it just on what is speculated to be going on internally within the subject of our observations, but it is on the approximation of the subject's (i.e., the patient's) psychic reality, and the associated affective states (Ornstein, 1979). Through the capacity to resonate, and to grasp the unique meanings of another person's experience, we arrive at what others feel. Empathy may be distinguished from sympathy in that in sympathy a merger occurs, but it leads to a loss of self boundaries and results in an identification with the subject.

Empathy has no inherent therapeutic value. In and of itself it is not curative. When used therapeutically empathy enhances the "holding environment," the atmosphere of acceptance, concern, and judicious involvement, and creates the conditions necessary for therapeutic work. The creation of an atmosphere in which the patient feels welcome, engaged in a process, and heard is not new to clinicians. It has been applied long before it became a precept of good therapeutic management. What is different about the empathic stance, as used here, is that observations and comments are made in the context of therapeutic compassion.

Clinicians are intent on understanding patients and on collecting data that are accurate and are reflective of the psychic reality of the patient (Saleeby, 1979). Yet many difficulties face a therapist in maintaining a consistent empathic stance: interferences are produced by the technique itself, by issues in the patient's reality, by the frequency of sessions, and by countertransference reactions. All these may interfere with the total immersion in the patient's experience. A sense of continuity is often difficult to maintain, and external or internal distractions can become resistances to the process. When a glimpse of the patient's inner state is obtained, the temptation to build stereotypic generalization of the dynamics is great. And rather than patiently await the sense of conviction that is attained through the total immersion in the patient's psyche which empathic introspection permits, therapists arrive at premature closures that may abort the process.

The systematic application of the empathic approach to the clinical situation has led to a new understanding of a number of disturbances, and to a powerful agent for the healing of the dysfunctional states.

PSYCHOPATHOLOGY: CONFLICT OR DEFICIT

Self psychology questions the proposition that conflict—between the drives and the environment or the ego—is the only motivating force in development and the only source for psychic disturbances.

Stolorow and Lachmann (1980) in their instructive book point out the differences between explanations drawn from ego psychology and those derived from self psychology. Their thesis is that it takes psychic structure for conflict to exist. The conflict model attributes much more structure to the infant than is warranted by our observations. The tripartite model, which is suitable for explaining oedipal pathology, is displaced backward to explain preoedipal problems. The hierarchy of defenses postulated in early ego development may be replaced by a much simpler set of explanations. The alternative explanation is that it is the deficiencies (in the sense of immaturities, or absence of development) of the young child that produce dysfunctional states. Rather than speaking of drives and ego, one can refer to the self as the construct most applicable to this early developmental state.

The child requires an empathic environment to be provided by nurturant objects. This gives the growing infant the sustenance necessary to develop its inborn sense of cohesion (Toplin, 1971). The absence of empathy leads to parental misperceptions of the child's needs, and to consequent failures to provide adequately for the child. The parents represent selfobjects, who complement the infant's immature self and provide functions the infant cannot provide. In this sense it is not so much the attachment that is meaningful, but the specifics of the infant's psychic reality needs, as provided by the selfobject, that are crucial. This view concretizes what has long been known: the child needs not just an average expectable response from the environment, but the very specific understanding of the individual lacunae.

Empathic failures lead to fragmentation and to interferences in the development of cohesion. These interferences lead to failures in structuralization. If the internalizations of self-regulating, self-soothing, and self-sustaining capacities either fail or are incomplete, a deficient sense of self results.

The disorders of the self then are disturbances that stem not from conflict states as such, but from deficits in the sense of self (Kohut & Wolf, 1978). These deficits may manifest as psychotic states in fragmentation-prone, noncohesive personalities, or as the so-called borderline states in personalities whose basic endowment is incomplete or on whom the environment has had a traumatic or disintegrative impact (Toplin, 1980). Or they may be evident in the narcissistic personality disorders whose disturbances result from a loss of cohesion secondary to a trauma, or who are the product of specific deficits in the self that find expression in symptomatic behaviors. Although the neurotic disturbances are best understood as resulting from internal conflict, they may also be seen as disturbances in the self that are the result of the hypercathexis of sexual or aggressive feelings, in response to empathic failures.

Conflict in such a scheme may refer to the attempts by a person to defend against the conscious or unconscious experiences of the pain engendered by the deficit itself. Or it may refer to states in which incompatible solutions to self deficits are sought.

THE GOALS OF TREATMENT

The self unfolds ontogenetically from infancy to maturity from an archaic (undeveloped) self to a mature cohesive self. It is composed of two poles, which, like a double helix, remain in a tension state with one another throughout the life span. The poles utilize and interact with a person's inborn gifts, talents, or limitations and handicaps. The result of those three components—the grandiose self, the idealized parent imago, and the inborn attributes—represents the enduring structures that, in part, define the content of the self. The self may also be defined as being composed of the totality of the subjective experiences—past and present, conscious and unconscious—of the person.

Treatment is conceptualized as directed to one of several goals: (1) to help a patient recover from a fragmenting experience (Goldberg, 1973); (2) to help the patient achieve a higher level of structuralization, either through the internalization of structures, or the development of a compensatory structure in lieu of the absent one; or (3) to achieve a level of coherence, continuity, and cohesion not previously attained (Goldberg, 1978).

The capacity to attain any of these goals is, of course, contingent upon the type of pathology, the level of development, and the investment a patient has in change. Perhaps the goals of treatment may best be understood by contrasting them with the goals of treatment in ego psychology. Structural theory proposes two sets of factors that are considered curative in the therapeutic process: identification, and conflict resolution through insight. Identifications occur in the course of supportive relationships, or in the course of growth-producing experiences, such as helping a patient achieve object constancy. On the other hand, insight into aspects of one's repressed past may lead to the recovery of memories that can assist the process of resolution. Working through is the means by which the hard-earned insights are integrated within the personality.

In self psychology the curative factors are the provision of the missing selfobject functions in cases where support is indicated, or the transmuting internalization of those functions with the achievement of a relative sense of autonomy as an independent center of initiative. In the latter case, the aim is the achievement of coherence, continuity, and cohesion. The change envisioned is to a higher level of integration and functioning, with the deficit corrected or adequately compensated. The latter may be attained through analysis or intensive psychotherapy.

The goal of reconstruction in self psychology is to find meaning and continuity in one's history, rather than to resolve the oedipal conflict, and to reconstruct the infantile experiences surrounding that phase. Since the psychic reality of the patient is more important than the actuality of what occurred in childhood, the emphasis of search is less on the recovery of traumatic events in the patient's past than on the patient's experience of these events and their meaning. The therapeutic result is the fitting together of the recollections into a coherent whole, which leads to a feeling of integration and strength. Having made sense of the inner turmoil, the patient finds it has subsided and a sense of inner peace is achieved (Cohler, 1979, 1980).

The excursions into one's self are not like archeological trips in which one attempts to dig up the past to recover the truth, or to discover what "really occurred." Such efforts only lead to the recovery of remnants of one's self. Rather the task can be likened to that of a historian seeking a plausible explanation for an historical event. It is like the writing of a memoir. The autobiographical aspects are recognized as a partial and subjective view of what occurred. No claim need be made of seeing the whole or of arriving at an objective account of the events. The establishment of the sense of continuity with one's past leads to the establishment of a linkage with one's heritage. Cohesion produced by this sense of continuity leads to a consonance of ambitions and ideals in the context of one's capacities. The sense of fulfillment of one's self and one's life goals is the therapeutic culmination of the intervention (Myerhoff, 1980; Spence, 1982).

The following case is an example of this approach.

> Jonathan was 16 years old when he came to treatment because of a serious problem with drug dependence. He was a very bright young, man, the son of highly successful professional parents. Until about two years prior to his entry into treatment, he had made a reasonably good adjustment. He then became involved with marijuana, then with LSD, and then with speed, ending up with a relatively indiscriminate use of whatever substance was available. He searched for the elusive experience that would give him the specific euphoric high he valued. Music was a large part of that experience, and was felt to enhance it.
>
> About six months into twice-a-week treatment, after the establishment of a positive transference and a therapeutic alliance, Jonathan decided to change his life-style and to give up drugs altogether. This was done without any urging on my part. In fact I had to caution him about the effects of such a sudden withdrawal, and the difficulties he would confront if he proceeded with his plan. He went ahead, however, and there followed a critical six-month period during which he struggled mightily with his dependence. He experienced episodes of severe depression, depersonalization, some visual hallucinations, and a sense of total isolation from the world of his former friends. At times we discussed possible hospitalization, but he opted against that and was able to weather the crises.
>
> By the end of the first year of treatment, he had recovered some of his lost functioning, and was able to manage a totally drugfree existence. By the second year, he was earning straight A's in his senior year in high school. The episode upon which I wish to focus occurred during this period. A silent idealizing transference solidly undergirded our work together as he and I examined the reasons for his turning to drugs in the first place. We were able to see that part of his problem was related to a precipitous deidealization of his powerful father early in adolescence when his father unjustly accused him of a variety of minor misdemeanors.

He related the following conversation with his father. They had been discussing existentialism, and he had asked his father what he thought of all that is ugly and repulsive in the world. He could not understand the place of violence in human existence. His father responded by saying that he dismissed these things as not affecting him, and was not troubled by them. Jonathan reported that he was appalled at his father's intellectual shallowness, although he knew his father also to be capable of profound scholarly work. He could only assume that his father was belittling him, and it was another example of why he no longer admired the man.

Since we had worked through that particular piece of dynamic previously, I felt that another issue was at stake here. I responded by saying that I could understand his disappointment and rage, but that I felt that at this point he was dealing with a different issue. I thought that the object of his anger and disillusionment was himself. The ugliness he spoke of represented that part of his history he had failed to explain to himself and would like to forget. His problem now was integrating that fact, and that when he turned to his father for a solution, he was also disappointed that his father could not help him. The task he and I faced was one of helping him to find meaning within the continuity of his sense of self. He smiled and related that the morning before the discussion with his father he had driven to the place in the woods that was his favorite when he would get high. With the stereo in his car turned on full blast and the car doors opened, he sat in the spot where he had had his last trip on acid. As he sat there, he had experienced a feeling of amazement that he used to do such things. He felt that his prior search had been so meaningless and so mindless that he could not believe he had participated in it. He felt glad to be in full touch with his feelings and his being, but the puzzle remained.

This young man's inner struggles did not reflect an inner conflict, but an attempt to acquire cohesion and continuity. While he may be seen as struggling with the issue of identification with his father, that was not the central issue in the transference at that moment. What was central was the division in his sense of self that barred him from feeling whole. The therapeutic task was to help heal that rift, and to permit him to see himself as at peace with his past.

TECHNIQUE AND SELF PSYCHOLOGY

A variety of technical issues are commonly encountered in this type of psychotherapeutic work that illustrate the workings of the empathic introspective point of view in the clinical situation.

Interventions are guided not only by theories of how change is achieved, but also by values that are implicit in the direction toward which change occurs. Whether change is considered to consist of symptomatic improvement, improvement in functioning, or more profound personality restructuring, the technique should be capable of accomplishing its goals. The following techniques spell out the ways in which the clinical goals of self psychology are brought about (Palaci, 1980).

The Psychotherapeutic Situation

The environment created in the work with patients is a major determinant of the success of the process. Winnicott has called this atmosphere, appropriately enough, the "holding environment" (Modell, 1976). The task for the therapist is to facilitate becoming a selfobject for the patient. The patient's readiness to accept this offer is dependent upon the patient's pathology, prior therapeutic experiences, and other variables. Some of the problems encountered by therapists illustrate the difficulties in maintaining this stance. The tact with which seemingly minor issues are handled may determine the course of therapy.

Example

In psychotherapy patients sit face to face with the therapist, thus permitting eye contact. The meaning of eye contact has never been discounted, and the general view in structural theory has been that good eye contact reflects good object relatedness. It was Freud's immense distaste for being looked at, in fact, that led to the use of the couch. Sullivan also made the avoidance of eye contact part of his technique.

The significance of the handling of this issue crystalized for me at a time when I was seeing two children and an adolescent, all of whom had been seen diagnostically by other therapists to whom they refused to return. The parents reported that the children's reason for not returning was that they had felt much discomfort at being "stared at" by the therapists. The issue for me was to uncover what that had meant to these patients. Were they poorly equipped to form object ties, or was some other dynamic at play that led them to resist the help that was offered? It occurred to me that, at least for some patients, the process of coming to therapy itself represents a narcissistic injury. The therapist's stare may trigger the sense of shame and embarrassment at being placed in a situation experienced as not in their control. In taking this approach, I have found that many children who were previously considered resistive to treatment are easily won over once their injury is acknowledged, and their embarassment minimized by less confrontative eye contact. The meaning of eye contact in ongoing treatment is illustrated in the following:

> A women patient in her mid-30s had problems centering around a set of childhood experiences in which her father, to whom she was close, died when she was nine, and her mother, who was inadequate and overwhelmed, could give her children little nurturance. The patient grew up partly by being cared for by a depressed older sister and partly by fending for herself. Her disturbance might be described as stemming from a failure in the internalization of an appropriately mirroring structure. In her treatment, which had been in process for a number of years, she had been unable to make eye contact with me except in the brief moment as she walked into the room. The rest of the session was spent with her looking anywhere in the office except at my face. As I reviewed my contacts with this patient, I found that rather than being impoverished in her object relationships, her life was filled with meaningful attachments. Furthermore, there was no doubt as to the intensity of the transference, and the meaning of her therapy to her. The issue of eye contact was related to a very different set of factors. The focal issue was one of shame. A deep sense of shame pervaded her life. Her feelings were ones of unworthiness of others' attention. And while she longed for the gaze of other people, she averted her eyes for fear she would be found wanting. This shift in diagnostic assessment led to a very different understanding of the transference meaning of her behavior. It led to the possibility of continued help, rather than to a possible stalemate.

This issue has implications for another group of patients who, in contrast, enjoy being looked at and admired. Here my attention was drawn by the frequent comments made by male therapists that some women act seductively toward them. This was considered a hazard especially in the treatment of adolescent girls by men. Since I see a large number of adolescents, I did not wish to preclude seeing young women or to consider this an insurmountable problem. I acccpt rcfcrrals of adolescents of both sexes and attend to my countertransferences. It was in the course of treating a particularly attractive female adolescent that I became aware of the so-called problem of seductiveness.

> This 16-year-old started coming to her sessions during the summer in appropriate but highly abbreviated forms of dress. Ordinarily one would consider them seductive. During these sessions I found myself struggling to avoid looking at her, feeling that were I to do so, she would regard my gaze as seductive. However, there was nothing in the therapeutic process that confirmed my countertransference. The concerns that had brought her into treatment were related to her feelings that she had an inordinate need for attention from her peers and her teachers, and unless this need was satisfied, she would feel depressed. When I did allow myself to look at her, what I became aware of was her yearning for admiration and affirmation. The yearnings that had become activated were not connected to object instinctual needs, but rather to the wish for a mirroring selfobject. Had I continued to avoid looking at her, or had I interpreted her behavior as seductive, I would have repeated her childhood injury and trauma of feeling unacceptable to her mother. Or alternatively the transference might have become eroticized and the injury would not have healed.

These may seem simple or subtle issues but they highlight an attitude toward patients that is essential to establishing, from the first moment of contact, an atmosphere based on an empathic understanding of the patient's needs. This attitude attends to the narcissistic vulnerabilities of patients and the minimizing of possible injury.

The Nature of Transference in Self Psychology

Freud (1914) originally defined transference as the process through which an impulse associated with an unconscious wish bypasses the defenses, crosses the repression barrier, and appears in consciousness in disguised form. This metapsychological definition was later modified to include a clinical definition in which transference was defined as the process through which the unconscious wishes originally directed at the parent figures are displaced onto the person of the analyst. The displacement leads to a distortion in the perception of the reality of the present-day object, and to thoughts and behaviors that represent the earlier infantile ties.

Clinicians of all persuasions, however, have gone far beyond this original definition. Reference is made not only to transference of drive wishes and impulses, but also to transference of superego contents, of defenses, and of ego states (Sandler et al., 1969). What is implied is that it is not only id contents that can be displaced, but also specific psychic structures. This distinction is crucial to the understanding of the nature of transference in self psychology. It is also the distinction between the dynamically repressed—the unconscious impulses defended against by the ego, and the descriptively repressed—the structures of the mind of which we ordinarily are unaware.

Transferences in self psychology refer to both unconscious, or repressed, wishes and longings that are directed to the selfobject, and to the displaced affects surrounding the deficits in the psychic structure. Thus in the selfobject transference, the selfobject becomes the embodiment of the longed-for empathic response the patient did not receive as a child. At the same time, it is the expression of the fear that the selfobject will respond as the original object had responded in childhood. In an idealizing transference, the patient fails to internalize the structures associated with phase-appropriate experiences of idealization of one or both parents. The trauma consists of an empathic failure that has thwarted the child's developmental needs. The pain associated with this trauma may be identified as a narcissistic injury. The injury may lead to a repression of the longings for the missed experiences and of the associated pain. The pain and longings, however, remain active in the patient's unconscious and renewed efforts are made to seek substitute selfobjects that promise to provide what was not internalized. It is this motive that expresses itself in the form of transferences to a therapist.

In the initial phases of treatment, a therapist may be faced with resistances to the exposure to this pain and the associated longings. These defenses may have to be worked through before evidence of transferences emerges. The nature of the mobilized transference depends upon the patient's pathology. A patient with a well-structuralized personality will present one of the major transferences described by Kohut: a mirror transference, or an idealizing transference. A patient with a less structured personality may present with a more diffuse or chaotic transference that reflects the structure of the patient's sense of self.

A 16-year-old young man was brought to me by his parents following their discovery that he was having an ongoing homosexual relationship with a stranger who had picked him up on the street. Initially the young man was quite resistive to involving himself with me. He tested my attitudes about homosexuality, insisting it was simply an expression of a sexual preference. I shared with him the fact that I held no prejudice about homosexuality and that my concern was less with that than with the fact that he had placed himself in a position in which he was endangering himself by picking up people on the street, and by having to hide from his parents a part of his life that must be very important to him. I suggested that under the circumstances he could not be feeling very good about himself. He hesitantly accepted that, and agreed to see me once a week. His parents, in the meantime, had extracted from him a promise that he would not engage in homosexual activities until he had resolved some of his problems in therapy. They were willing to accept his homosexuality, but only if they were convinced that he had given the matter considerable thought and discussed it with a professional.

As the treatment unfolded, and he was able to reveal to me that he had no intention of keeping his promise to his parents, he continued to engage in homosexual practices with a variety of partners—although he was more cautious in his choices. The pattern that emerged was one in which he would seek out sexual excitement whenever he felt depressed or depleted. As he had few friends although he was extremely bright, he felt isolated from his environment, and his sexual activity seemed related to his efforts to seek out selfobjects to attenuate the pain of his isolation. The father of this young man was a gruff, hot-tempered man whose brusk demeanor was in sharp contrast to his son's somewhat delicate disposition and effete manner. My patient, while longing for an idealizing relationship with his father, felt totally alienated from him. His father, for example, worshipped the power of a good car, whereas the son saw in it only a means of transportation. His father prized physical prowess and aggression whereas the son had a nonviolent approach to life. The mother was a theatrical woman for whom dress and makeup were serious matters that required a great deal of attention. She valued femininity in its most stereotypic forms. The patient clearly felt more comfortable in his mother's world than in that of his father. Not surprisingly the transference that evolved was a mother transference along the mirroring line of development. This manifested itself in his preoccupation with appearance and the exhibitionistic forms of dress he chose to wear. He would come in proudly, showing off some new article of clothing. He often shopped in the Salvation Army used clothing store, where he would buy old-fashioned items and flaunt them for the world to see. Interestingly, what he chose was very much in the avant-garde of men's fashion of the day.

The session of particular interest here took place after six months of treatment. His parents were out of town and could not accompany him. He had been staying with his grandmother for the week and so had missed an appointment. On the weekend following the missed appointment, he related the following episode. He decided he needed some excitement because he felt bored. He went to a shopping mall, was picked up by a sailor, and ended up in a motel. He spoke of the details of the sexual encounter in a manner that was different from the descriptions he had previously given of such encounters. He said that during the mutual masturbation and oral-genital sexual activity he found himself disgusted by the man's unwashed state, by his tattoos, and by his muscular appearance. It was the antithesis of what he fantasized about a sexual experience. I empathized with his disappointment at not finding the excitement he had sought, but focused on the search for excitement and on the events that led to the search for the experience in the first place. He soon revealed that while part of him was glad that his parents had been away, he had missed being home. He had also missed coming to his session since there were things about which he had planned to talk with me. He felt a sense of discouragement at the thought that they would be forgotten by the time he came for his next session. I commented that he sounded depressed, and that he had mistaken boredom for feeling empty and lonely. He agreed when I suggested that the sexual excitement he sought served the purpose both of avoiding the pain of his depression and of achieving the contact with and affirmation from another person that he constantly needed.

In this case the transference was well structuralized and the dynamics emerged clearly. Diagnostically this is an indication of a disorder of the self in which the deficit is contained within a relatively well-encompassed area of the self. The young man may thus be seen as suffering a narcissistic behavior disorder. Were he more disturbed, it is possible that the relationship and transference would have been more chaotic.

Countertransference and Abstinence

The term "countertransference" has been used to describe the therapist's inappropriate responses to patients, the therapist's transference to the patient stemming from unresolved issues in the therapist's past, and the therapist's responses to material evoked by the patient's own transferences. Every therapist must own having countertransference reactions that are part of the therapeutic process, and this is the countertransference dealt with here.

The basic assumption is that in the course of being exposed to another person's intense transferences, therapists find that responses are evoked in themselves that have considerable significance in work with patients. The uses made of these responses discriminate between therapists and their different styles. For some the responses are seen as a set of data important to track, and on which comments or interpretations are made. For others the responses serve as cues for interventions that may include concrete actions the therapist feels need to be taken. Whether or not it is appropriate to share with a patient the thoughts and feelings aroused in the therapist as countertransference remains controversial. The matter becomes even more complicated with patients who insist that the therapist tell what he or she thinks, or who demand some action by the therapist that may be felt to be beyond the bounds of the basic rules of psychotherapy. The criteria according to which abstinence from certain forms of communication or action is to be judged are far from clear. For example, a patient may insist on knowing whether the therapist is married or has children, or may insist that the therapist attend a graduation or a wedding, or may offer a gift that must be accepted. The principles by which therapists ought to be guided have yet to be spelled out in any detail. It is true that general statements have been made that more clearly apply to psychoanalytic treatment than to psychotherapy, but these tend to be in the form of broad prohibitions rather than guidelines.

The topics of countertransference and abstinence are discussed together because of their interrelatedness and because a common set of countertransference reactions is encountered on the issue of whether or not to gratify a patient's request. It is often difficult to decide whether the therapist is acting out—on the basis of the therapist's own needs—or is truly responding to the patient's pleas.

The common countertransference reactions to the disturbances of the self have been described by Kohut (1971). In summary they usually entail feelings of boredom and of not being appreciated as a separate person in cases of the mirror transferences, and feelings of power and grandiosity associated with the idealizing transferences. In the less structured disturbances where feelings of fragmentation and disconnectedness predominate in the patient, these are responded to by feelings of anxiety and bewilderment in the therapist. The less benign forms of countertransference involve the therapist's taking the patient as a selfobject. Thus the therapist acts out the patient's idealization by self-aggrandizing behaviors; or acts out the patient's need for mirroring by actual praise or criticism. Acting on any of these feelings leads a therapist to repeat with the patient the latter's traumatic past. Recognizing with the patient the nature of the experience, on the other hand, is the first step toward an eventual alleviation of the distress. Thus, gratifying the longings by actually mirroring a patient through praise or compliments, or gratifying the longings for an idealized selfobject by, in fact, playing the role of omnipotent therapist, are contraindicated with the more structuralized disorders.

In some situations, however, the therapist's counterreaction is stirred to the point of feeling that it is indeed appropriate that some action be taken, that it might be untherapeutic to withhold such a response from the patient. For example, as therapists we have no quarrel with the position that in extreme cases, in which patients threaten harm to themselves or others, some direct intervention is indicated. In less extreme cases, as in the treatment of children, we acknowledge the therapeutic value of limiting a child's behavior, even if the child has to be physically restrained if it is felt that the child is about to get out of control or become overstimulated. With adolescents we find ourselves acquiescing to requests to call a parent or a teacher under special circumstances, even when there is no threat of physical harm. If these examples are not always indicative of the therapist's countertransference, then they must be understood as reflective of an empathic understanding of underlying dynamics in the therapeutic process. I am suggesting that whenever a therapist feels so moved as to find it necessary to act upon such a request, and that it is absolutely clear in the therapist's mind that the gratification of the request does not represent a need of the therapist's own, then the meaning of the interaction must be understood differently than as acting out. The interaction at that point is indicative of the patient's selfobject needs—whether regressive or archaic—having reached a level of intensity and urgency that is overwhelming. In addition the patient does not have the necessary structures to cope with those needs and is desirous of having the therapist provide them.

The patient is, therefore, expecting the therapist to be the missing structure and to do literally for the patient what the patient cannot do. The threat of loss of cohesion then leads the therapist to respond to the patient in whatever manner is appropriate. What this implies is that diagnostically the patient at that moment is functionally on the border between integration and psychotic disintegration. In such cases of less structuralized disorders, it is necessary, in fact, to gratify a patient's request or longings since the goal of treatment is less one of achieving internalization than of providing a corrective experience.

> A young woman patient of 24 suffered from feelings of depletion and chronic depression. She felt her life to have little meaning; her isolation was oppressive. She felt disconnected from the world. During such periods of isolation, her anxiety would mount to the point where she experienced feelings of unreality, and she would become actively suicidal. Her therapy was seen as a link to reality. My presence was experienced as an affirmation of her as a human being. At one point in the treatment, she had managed to break out of the shell in which she lived sufficiently to get a job in a flower shop. She soon felt appreciated and experienced a new sense of enjoyment. In her desire to have me be a part of that experience, she invited me to stop at the shop and visit her in the surroundings in which she now felt comfortable. My assenting to her request was seen by me as a therapeutic gesture that provided her with a much needed acknowledgment of her self-worth. To have refused the request, or to even have delayed fulfilling it until the dynamics were fully clarifying, would have constituted a shattering rebuff. The visit was made and the treatment progressed.

The countertransference feelings were also related to my own wishes to rescue this patient from her desolation and isolation. This feeling was compounded by the fear that in her desperation she would attempt suicide. She had on several occasions talked of taking her life as a way out of her meaningless existence. The response evoked must be understood as diagnostically indicative of the level of other selfobject needs—the more intensely experienced, the more indicative of the extent of the deficit.

> Another patient, a 32-year-old artist who was just beginning treatment, revealed in the early hours a childhood memory of an event that had haunted him since its occurrence. He had never forgotten it, or repressed it, and yet he was not quite sure of its meaning. He remembered being seven years old at the time, and coming home excited by some piece of news he had seen headlined in a newspaper. He had run to his mother, who was an illiterate immigrant. The news he had to tell her was that war had broken out. He boastfully went on to say that when he grew up he would see to it that such things as wars would never happen. She responded gruffly, telling him to stop talking nonsense, and that he would be better off concerning himself with cleaning up his room. He remembered feeling devastated. The memory, of course, was seen by me as representing a screen memory of multiple injuries of a similar nature.
>
> Two weeks after relating this memory, he brought to his session a large portfolio of photographs, writings, letters, and other mementos of his younger days. He waited until the end of the session to show me its contents, and turning it over to me as the precious possession it was for him, he asked if I would look at it. Since there was no time left, I suggested he leave it with me until the following session. Eyeing me carefully, he agreed. When he returned the following time, he could not wait to hear what I thought about his material. I said that I was touched by the fact that he wanted to share this with me, and went on to comment on a number of the items that struck me as significant. To have avoided gratifying his wish for affirmation would have constituted a repetition of the childhood trauma. Yet it seemed too early to plunge into an interpretation of the meaning of his request, since that too would have constituted an injury. I was left with the only choice—to gratify his wish and demonstrate to him that I could function for him as a different selfobject than his mother.

Nature of Therapeutic Interventions

Since the primary vehicle of psychotherapeutic work is the set of verbal interchanges between patient and therapist, we must place the role of these interchanges into perspective. Much may be said about the role of words in the modality we use. We refer to interpretations, confrontations, clarifications, and similar interventions as techniques we use to achieve specific results. Yet the words alone do not constitute the essence of treatment. In fact, by attending too closely to the words a therapist may not hear the accompanying melody.

Interventions occur in the context of a process. What is said by the patient or the therapist reflects, in part, the content of what is transpiring. We, of course, are aware of the latent, preconscious, or unconscious contents of our patients' communications. We are attuned to the affective tones that underly these communications. Yet at a still different level, the process involves another type of interaction. This interaction may be referred to as the merger between the patient and therapist that binds the two into a working unit. This merger may be thought of, in Mahler's terms, as a loss of defined boundaries between the participants in the process. Or it may be conceptualized as the complementarity that comes to exist between the two. Klein would refer to this as the part-object function the therapist comes to have for the patient, and Winnicott might speak of the therapist fulfilling a transitional object function for the patient. All of these approximate, but do not entirely convey, what in self psychology is referred to as the merger with the selfobject.

The selfobject in the transference represents those functions the patient never internalized. Verbalizations may be used either to facilitate or to impede the process itself. There are three distinct uses to which interpretations may be made.

1) Interpretations may be directed at the defenses a patient first uses to avoid exposing the painful affects the deficits have created. In this sense interpretations may be understood as being directed at the resistances the patient has to developing a transference, and to forming a merger with the therapist.

2) Subsequent to the unfolding of the transference, interpretations may be directed at explaining to the patient the selfobject function the therapist has come to have for the patient.

3) Interpretations may attempt to reconstruct the genetic roots of a patient's specific deficits that give him or her the sense

of historical continuity that is a necessary part of self-cohesion and self-esteem.

It is clear that interpretation is being used in a different sense than that traditionally used in ego psychology. The reference is not to uncovering unconscious derivatives of instinctual impulses, or to lifting the repression with a view to helping arrive at a resolution of a conflict. Rather the comments that are called interpretations are directed at maintaining an optimal merger within which the therapeutic work is conducted. These comments serve to facilitate the transmuting internalization of the missing functions. Several implications flow from this. First, the distinction traditionally made between insight therapy and supportive therapy need no longer be maintained as sharply as it once was. We can take a unitary view of the therapeutic stance. The stance of the therapist is the same for both modalities. Second, insight is not a precondition to structuralization or internalization. Since the merger itself provides an undergirding support to the patient, and since internalizations occur as a result of the optimal frustrations of the merger experience, the verbalization of the contents of the process may aid the process but are not a precondition for its development. Third, the therapist can consistently stay within the transference material, and within the intrapsychic experience of the patient, and not need to step out to the realities that confront the patient, no matter what the diagnosis.

A widow in her late 40s came into treatment following the unmourned death of an idealized husband four years prior. She was angry, depressed, and functioning poorly. Since her husband's death, she had made a bad marriage, which she had terminated within a year.

The treatment process did not follow the traditional lines of mourning for a loss. Instead it dealt with the massive deidealization of the dead husband, which had impeded a proper adaptation. Her husband, who was a social worker, had had two coronaries and had managed to deny the prospect of his own death. He had never been able to discuss with her that eventuality. She felt betrayed more than bereft.

She was seen on a once-a-week basis and a transference developed that was never interpreted or commented upon. Rather than idealize me as the displaced figure of the lost husband, she required instead my silent mirroring of her terrible plight. She could not impress upon me sufficiently how terrible things were for her now. While it was clear that she had idealized her husband and that he had relished her admiration of him, she seemed more fulfilled by the feeling of having been chosen by such an admirable man. Her vulnerability lay in the fact that she did not have sufficient self-cohesion to feel sustained by her own accomplishments, but felt that she could only be a person by virtue of whom she had married.

As treatment progressed over a period of a year and a half, great symptomatic improvement took place. Her functioning, which was nearly at a standstill when she started treatment, returned to the high level she had attained prior to her first marriage. She reported a new sense of freedom and competence she had not felt in a long time. From her perspective, treatment seemed to be nothing more than talking to a good friend. She felt supported and understood. From my perspective I felt, in the countertransference, touched by someone whose life had been shattered by an untimely death, and whose sense of self had so depended on her marital partner that she could not remain cohesive without him. She felt isolated, enraged, and bewildered by her helplessness. The gains that were made were the result of the merger with me, and the sustaining effect that merger had upon her. Nothing more needed to be done or said to improve upon what was already happening in the treatment.

Termination

In analysis a classic termination was always considered incomplete unless a mourning process was evidenced. It is a clinical fact that many of my patients do not experience either rage or a mourning reaction when treatment is ended. In *The Restoration of the Self* (Kohut, 1977) and in "Letter to the Author: Preface to *Lehrjahre Auf Der Couch by Tilmann Moser* (Ornstein, 1978), Kohut points out that termination not only need not entail mourning, but may be experienced with prideful triumph. If the process of therapy entails the development of missing structure, all there really is to mourn is the lost and wasted years that preceded the restoration of one's self, and not those shadowy figures of one's oedipal past. The studies of children's losses through death have led me to view the process of mourning from a somewhat different perspective than the traditional one (Palombo, 1981). One must consider not only the impact of the loss as entailing the detachment from someone who was perceived as a separate center of initiative, but also as inflicting a narcissistic loss. However, these reactions are found only in those situations in which the relationship continues to serve selfobject needs in the present. When the selfobject needs are no longer as active and the relationship has produced transmuting internalization, the loss may be experienced as the logical conclusion of the life cycle and is accepted without much grief. Consider, for example, the reaction to the loss of son or daughter versus the reaction to the loss of aged grandparents. Even though the attachment may have been as intense at times, the latter loss is not experienced as painfully as the first, not because one felt less attached or less ambivalent toward the object, but because the selfobject functions were not as active.

This leads to the conclusion that grief and mourning are not necessarily seen in every instance of loss of a love object, but rather are to be expected in instances where the selfobject ties continue to be present. When the attachment is to an object that formerly served a selfobject function but where the function has become transmutingly internalized, then the loss of the object is not mourned. We do not mourn our graduations and our moves to higher developmental levels, but celebrate them even though they may entail detachments from loved objects. Terminations, when viewed from this perspective, lead to very different sets of expectations than we formerly had for this process (Palombo, 1982).

In classic psychoanalytic theory, one could not speak of a proper termination unless a resolution of the oedipal conflict had occurred and mourning for the lost incestuous ties could follow. Since this outcome was seldom expected in psychotherapy, the ending of treatment was not considered to constitute a proper termination, but an interruption.

Terminations of psychotherapy fall into two types: those in which the termination comes prior to the completion of the process of internalization of the missing selfobject functions, and those in which the internalizations were achieved. In the first case, since the termination in effect represents a rupture in the process by virtue of the fact that the patient's deficits continue to be present, rage reactions and grief may be present (Kohut, 1972). These may not manifest themselves in situations in which the patient has displaced those needs onto figures outside of treatment and has found satisfaction in other relationships.

This implies that mourning and grief are evidence of the need for continued therapeutic work, rather than of the completion of the work. The pain represents the absence of internalization, and a reconcretization of the therapeutic selfobject may result. This is seen as a regressive attempt at holding onto the functions the patient does not yet feel exist within him or herself (Goldberg, 1975).

For those patients who have developed the capacity to hold onto what they have internalized, the termination is experienced as a release, and as the accomplishment of a task. It is an occasion for happiness rather than sadness, for celebration rather than mourning (Palombo, 1981).

CONCLUSIONS

Over the years social casework and clinical social work have developed a wide variety of approaches to achieve the goal of therapeutic intervention on behalf of troubled people. The distinctiveness of clinical social work lies in its emphasis on the individual in the context of the environment without negating the significance of that environment. Many divergent views have come into being. Perhaps the only binding theme in all these is a theory of change and a faith in human beings' capacity to bring about change in others as well as in themselves. Each point of view has borrowed generously from other disciplines, and each point of view has elaborated practice principles through which the goals of treatment may be achieved.

Psychoanalytic theory has been a major wellspring from which clinicians have drawn. From it have sprung the functional school, the ego supportive schools, and the psychosocial school. As psychoanalytic theory has been modified, the modifications have been incorporated into clinical social work general practice.

The advent of self psychology offers a further opportunity for advancement in the area of clinical practice. There is much in self psychology that is applicable to clinical social work. Its starting point is more humanistic and less biological than other approaches. Its creation of a therapeutic context gives more recognition to the healthier aspects of the personality than to psychopathology. Above all it affirms the goal of self-fulfillment within the context of values and ideals that have historical meaning to each individual.

The emphasis in treatment is, therefore, not only the resolution of a conflict based on infantile ties, but also the achievement of an optimal tension state between ambitions and ideals within the framework of one's native talents and basic endowments. This emphasis generates a set of practice principles that are well suited to the population we serve.

REFERENCES

Cohler, B. J. 1979. Adult development psychology and reconstruction in psychoanalysis. In *The course of life*, S. I. Greenspan and G. H. Pollock (Eds.). Washington D.C. U.S. Government Printing Office.

———. 1980. Developmental perspectives on the psychology of early childhood. In *Advances in self psychology*, A. Goldberg (Ed.). New York: International Universities Press, pp. 69–115.

Freud, S. 1937. Construction in analsyis. *Standard edition*, vol xxiii. London: Hogarth Press, pp. 255–270.

———. 1914. The dynamics of transference. *Standard edition*, vol xii. London: Hogarth Press. pp. 97–108.

Goldberg, A. 1973. The psychotherapy of narcissistic injuries. *Arch. Gen. Psychiatry* 28:722–726.

———, (Ed.). 1978.*The psychology of the self: A casebook*. New York: International Universities Press.

———, (Ed.). 1980. *Advances in self psychology*. New York: International Universities Press.

———, 1975. Narcissism and the readiness for psychotherapy termination. *Arch. Gen. Psychiatry* 32:695–699.

Hollis, F. 1980. Revisiting social work. *Soc. Casework* 61:3–10.

———. 1970. The psychosocial approach to casework practice. In *Theories of social casework*, Roberts and Nee (Eds.). Chicago: University Press.

Kohut, H. 1959. Introspection, empathy and psychoanalysis. *J. Am. Psychoanal. Assoc.* 7:459–483.

———. 1971. *The analysis of the self*. New York: International Universities Press.

———. 1977. *The restoration of the self*. New York: International Universities Press.

———. 1979. The two analyses of Mr. Z. *Int. J. Psycho-Anal.* 60:3–27.

———. 1972. Thoughts on narcissism and narcissistic range. In *Psychoanalytic study of the child*. New York: International Universities Press, pp. 360–400.

Kohut, H. and E. Wolf. 1978. The disorders of the self and their treatment: An outline. *Int. J. Psycho-Anal.* 59:413–426.

London, N. 1980. Discussion of Palaci, "Psychoanalysis of the self and psychotherapy." In *Advances in self psychology*, A. Goldberg (Ed.). New York: International Universities Press, pp. 337–347.

Modell, A. H. 1976. The holding environment and the therapeutic action of psychoanalysis. *J. Am. Psychoanal. Assoc.* 24:285–308.

Myerhoff, B. 1980. Telling one's story. *Center Mag.* 13(2):22–40.

Ornstein, P. (Ed.). 1978. *The search for the self.* New York: International Universities Press, Vol. I, II.

———. 1979. Remarks on the Central position of empathy in psychoanalysis. *Bull. Assoc. Psychonal. Med.* 18:95–108.

Palaci, J. 1980. Psychoanalysis of the self and psychotherapy. In *Advances in self psychology*, A. Goldberg (Ed.). New York: International Universities Press, pp. 317–335.

Palombo, J. 1981. Parent loss and childhood bereavement. *Clin. Soc. Work J.* 9(1):3–33.

———. 1982. Termination of psychotherapy. *Clin. Soc. Work J.* 10(2):15–27.

———. 1976. Theories of narcissism as related to social work practice. *Clin. Soc. Work J.* 4:147–161.

Perlman, H. H. 1970. The problem-solving model in social casework. In *Theories of social casework*, Roberts and Nee (Eds.). Chicago: University Press, pp. 129–180.

Saleeby, D. 1979. The tension between research and practice: Assumptions of the experimental paradigm. *Clin. Soc. Work J.* 7:267–284.

Sandler, J., et al. 1969. Notes on some theoretical and clinical aspects of transference. *Int. J. Psycho-Anal.* 50:633–645.

Simon, B. 1970. Social casework theory: An overview. In *Theories of social casework*, Roberts and Nee (Eds.). Chicago: University Press, pp. 352–398.

Smalley, R. E. The functional approach to casework practice. In *Theories of social casework*, Roberts and Nee (Eds.). Chicago: University Press, pp. 77–128.

Stolorow, R., and F. Lachmann. 1980. *Psychoanalysis of the developmental arrests: Theory and treatment.* New York: International Universities Press.

Spence, D. P. 1982. *Narrative truth and historical truth.* New York: W. W. Norton.

Thomas, E. J. Behavioral modification and casework. In *Theories of social casework*, Roberts and Nee (Eds.). Chicago: University Press, pp. 181–218.

Tolpin, M. 1971. On the beginnings of a cohesive self. In *Psychoanal. study of the child*. New York: International Universities Press, pp. 283–315.

Tolpin, P. 1980. The borderline personality: Its makeup and analyzability. In *Advances in self psychology*, A. Goldberg (Ed.). New York: International Universities Press, pp. 299–316.

Wolf, E. 1976. Ambience and abstinence. In the *Annual of psychoanalysis*. New York: International Universities Press.

DISCUSSION

Eda Goldstein

My admiration for Palombo's many contributions to our field, makes the expected role of the discussant as provocateur a challenge. To meet this challenge, I must return to the world of ego psychology and object relations theory from the land of self psychology to which we have been transported by a very skillful guide. To coin a phrase, although it was a very nice place to visit, I am uncertain about whether I want to live and practice there, at least all the time. I liked visiting because the patients with narcissistic pathology whom Palombo described reflected stable and cohesive idealizing and mirror transferences with which it was relatively easy to empathize. They did not present shifting and contradictory self and object representations in the transference, nor did they show persistent fluctuations between idealization and devaluation accompanied by intense rage and self-destructive behavior to threaten the treatment. They did not manifest problems in developing a therapeutic alliance, nor did they make persistent attempts to destroy human relationships and therapeutic efforts.

In self psychology land, narcissistic pathology is born of arrests in the developmental line of the self, which is viewed as existing apart from the messy underworld of libidinal and aggressive instincts and the structural derivatives of internalized object relations. It is a land in which narcissistic pathology is not a defensive structure. Thus it is a land where pathological defenses such as splitting of the object world and of the self and object representations into all good and all bad do not exist. I enjoyed visiting a place where the therapeutic task was developing coherence, continuity, and cohesiveness through empathic introspection and interpretation. This offered welcome respite from having to empathize with and help individuals acknowledge, accept, and integrate the aggressively tinged self and object representations characteristic of so many patients in the ego psychological–object relations universe. It was nice to have a rest, too, from a preoccupation with systematic assessments of the patient's past developmental history, past and current level of ego functioning, defenses, interpersonal relationships, and social context, and instead devote myself to a genuine encounter with the patient's subjective experience in the transference.

I raise these points not because I am convinced that one land is better than the other, but to highlight fundamental differences between Kohut's self psychology and Kernberg's integration of ego psychology with object relations theory in trying to understand and help patients with narcissistic pathology. In fact as a clinician I am struck by the fact that patients seem to reside in one land or the other, although they sometimes move from one to the other. As yet there is no theoretical bridge that can help us to explain how two differing theoretical perspectives dealing with the same pathology can both be right, and thus both be wrong.

Some authors have suggested that the major difference between these two theoretical and clinical perspectives is that while both deal with patients who are diagnosed as having narcissistic pathology, each emanates from therapeutic work with different patient populations. Since the patient groups vary in structural and functional levels, they appear in radically different ways in treatment. Others have argued that the very hypotheses and techniques of each theoretical system determine the nature of the clinical data that are observed. Thus Ornstein has argued that Kernberg's confrontation and interpretation of behavior that he views as reflecting primitive defensive operations actually create the aggressive reactions that Kernberg sees as central to the core pathology. Stolorow and Lachmann also have emphasized what they describe as the iotrogenic or therapist-induced effects produced by therapeutic techniques such as confrontation and interpretation of defenses, based on a view of narcissistic pathology as a defensive structure rather than as a developmental arrest. Palombo states that the ego psychological perspective places the therapist in the role of adversary to the patient's resistances, a role he views as problematic. On the other hand, Kernberg has argued that the truly empathic stance by the therapist requires that he or she be a "container" for the totality of the patient's inner experience, and that this necessitates helping the patient to recognize and integrate the aggressive as well as libidinal aspects of self and object representations. Kernberg cautions that what is called empathic on the part of the self psychologists may reflect an empathy with only one aspect of the patient, the part that is most comfortable for the patient to accept—namely, the patient's idealizing tendencies, yearning for the empathic parent, and fear of frustration once more. Thus the therapist may unwittingly reinforce the patient's splitting and lack of identity integration while fostering a primitive idealization of the therapist that obstructs the patient's ability to become more connected with the totality of inner experience. Kernberg argues that a fundamental flaw in self psychology is the assumption that the patient has a cohesive, though archaic and narcissistically vulnerable, self that reflects itself in a stable transference. He views the narcissistic patient as having a pathological grandiose self as a defensive structure. While in some higher level patients, this may give the appearance of integration, there is an underlying absence of what he calls identity integration in all narcissistic personalities, in whom overt or covert borderline structure is always present.

The therapeutic task in both systems of thought is similar, to help the patient develop more cohesion, continuity, and coherence. Thus each attempts to promote increased structuralization. In Kernberg's formulation, however, the pathological defensive structure that the patient strives to maintain to protect him or herself from conflict must give way in order for such cohesion to occur. Thus any effort to help the patient become aware of the defensive functioning is experienced as a threat. At the same time, such efforts are ego strengthening in the long run.

One of the most important features of Kohut's work in general and of the Palombo chapter in particular is the welcome focus on empathic introspection. This serves to counteract the view of the therapist as subject and the patient as object that has at times resulted from traditional psychoanalytic practice. Empathic introspection generates the climate in which the patient becomes free to engage in the therapeutic process, and creates the necessary conditions for the emergence of transfererence paradigms; it becomes the means by which the more structuralized patients develop transmuting internalizations, and the vehicle through which the less structuralized patients can experience correctives. In the Kohution formulation so exquisitely described here, an idealizing or mirror transference will emerge. In such an atmosphere the patient seeks in the therapist someone who will embody the longed-for empathic response the patient did not receive as a child, while at the same time expressing the fear that the therapist will respond as the original parent had responded in childhood. Presumably the inevitable failures of empathy in the therapeutic relationship will create disruptions, but the empathic understanding of these can lead to more optimal internalization, and growth.

A number of problems arise in trying to apply this perspective to narcissistic patients with overt borderline structures. First, these patients often do not develop stable transferences since the lack of integration of their internalized objects is reproduced in the transference. Thus the patient's attitude toward the therapist shifts dramatically, often unbeknown to the therapist, as in the following example.

Ms. B. is a 19-year-old hospitalized female who was diagnosed as having narcissistic personality in an overt borderline personality organization. She had been treated previously in private practice by a well-regarded analyst in three-times-a-week psychotherapy, and according to the analyst was a rewarding patient. When he was away on a three-day vacation, the patient overdosed and was almost comatose when her mother, coming home unexpectedly, found her. While hospitalized the patient described the analyst as stupid, cold, and too involved in his own ego to understand her. In the hospital she was treated by a young male psychiatrist with whom she was the good patient. She acknowledged feeling extremely lucky that she was assigned as his patient, attributing to him special sensitivity and empathic capacity. At the end of each session, she seemed to glow and would talk of getting more in touch with her feelings than ever before. The psychiatrist felt pleased, until he received a telephone call from the nursing staff one evening that the patient had been caught attempting to overdose. When he met with the nursing staff and social worker the next day, he learned that in the past week, unbeknown to him, the patient had constantly devalued him to the staff, patients, and her mother. She complained bitterly of his lack of experience and insensitivity.

In this case there was a failure of empathy but its origins did not lie in what was present in the therapeutic relationship but in what was absent and actively being kept out of it. A real part of the patient reflected that the correct empathic stance in this case required a more active exploration of the totality of the patient's experience. Palombo has referred to the importance of the search for meaning rather than for evidence in therapeutic work. Yet in this example the full meaning of the patient's transference reactions can only be understood when all the evidence of what is occurring in the here and now is brought into the treatment. It is crucial to bring such contradictory aspects of the patient's thoughts, feelings, and behavior into focus. The techniques for doing this have been called confrontation, an unfortunate term, because it connotes an angry assault, particularly when it is contrasted with empathy. Who can be against empathy, and who can be for an assaultive technique? My understanding of confrontation, however, is that it is a technique in which the therapist merely poses the patient with both sides of his or her contradictory behavior, feelings, or thought content and asks him or her to reflect on them. That this may be experienced by the patient as a threat stems from the patient's need to protect him or herself from conflict generated by the coming together of these contradictions, which the patient seeks to maintain.

This case example also points up the limitations growing out of reliance on the transference as the only source of clinical data. Important aspects of the case were active outside of the treatment situation. Issues of collaboration become more critical with such patients, but such arrangements are easier to manage on an inpatient unit or in a residential treatment environment than they are in outpatient or private practice. Decisions need to be made as to how to structure contact with significant others in the patient's life in many of these cases. Such additional parameters of treatment become particularly critical for patients who are impulsive and who engage in self-destructive behavior, as a reaction either to empathic failures in the transference, or to fluctuations of transference dispositions.

In his case examples, Palombo draws our attention in a very poignant way to the therapeutic value of gratifying selective patient requests. He sensitively identifies those patients who have less structuralized disorders, and for whom the goal of treatment is more to provide a corrective experience than to achieve internalization. In this respect the approach is similar to that of the Blancks, who advocate ego-building techniques that include such giving based on a careful understanding of the particular separation-individuation subphase deficiencies. It should be emphasized, however, that the powerful transference dispositions of narcissistic patients and the resultant countertransference reactions that develop necessitate safeguards for both patient and therapist. Patient efforts to obtain nurturance from and control the therapist directly make it critical that there be a systematic understanding of the patient's developmental level based on a careful inquiry into past and present functioning. Such diagnostic understanding can serve as the contextual framework in which the therapist can feel free to be creative in the therapeutic relationship. In this connection I find the self psychologists' lack of attention to descriptive and developmental diagnosis in favor of empathic introspection as the primary diagnostic and treatment tool a puzzling and unfortunate omission. We seem to be gaining one tool while losing another when we need to be using everything we know in the service of understanding and helping these challenging patients.

4 *The Witches: Mothers in Therapy*

Florence Lieberman

The second-class treatment often afforded mothers by mental health professionals is addressed. Lieberman theorizes that the root cause is society's need for an omnipotent being and the mental health establishment's need to create the mother ideal in the form of the "all-good mother." Examples from mythological lore, psychoanalytic theory, and clinical practice support her argument. A detailed case example of the author's work illustrates her technique and the countertransference analysis required, particularly when the therapist is a mother herself.

DISCUSSION by Lucille Spira Spira expands the reader's perception of the challenges to working with mothers through a reexamination of the case, further elaborating the discussion of the dynamics, and by offering examples of mothers who by virtue of their own internal worlds cannot connect with their infants in even the most basic way. The existence of programs designed by practitioners sensitively to address the needs of mothers is noted.

New studies about women are proliferating in the popular press and the sociological, psychological, and psychoanalytic literature. These attempt to clarify female growth, development, problems, and needs; they study women's differences from and similarities to men. In addition inequities for women with regard to opportunity, employment, and income are documented. Though open acknowledgment of these issues is a step forward, efforts to correct abuses often seem to approximate walking through quicksand.

The awareness of the predominance of men in the medical profession, despite an increase in the number of women physicians, and concern about tendencies toward "condescending, paternalistic, judgmental and non-informative" attitudes (Boston Women's Health Book Collective, 1971) have led many women to demand appropriate, instead of sexist, medical care; many are turning to women physicians for help.

In the field of psychotherapy, male psychotherapists have been criticized for having double standards for "normal" behavior, one for men and another for women. A few have been implicated in exploiting their female clients through unprofessional seduction and sexual activities. As a result many women prefer to consult women psychotherapists.

MOTHERS AND THE THERAPEUTIC ENCOUNTER

There is a group of women in double jeopardy—these are *MOTHERS*. They share the problems of all women, but in addition are exposed to abuse by therapists of both sexes. Two women clients of the same age, personality, and situation, except that one is a mother, are often viewed and treated differently, even when the mother's child is not the focus of attention. Of course these difficulties are compounded for the mother when the child *is* the primary client. It is as if, once a woman is identified as a mother, she loses entitlement to individuality, uniqueness, and personal need. She is categorized as a different type of human being.

The category, "mothers" is dichotomized into two groups: the ideal, acceptable mothers, and all others, or those who deviate from this ideal. The deviants are rarely understood or treated empathically. Instead they, too often, are reacted to as if they were wicked witches and repulsive clients. This splitting is reflected in many areas, including the treatment situation; and it is as likely to occur in social agencies where women professionals predominate as in the male psychotherapists's office.

"Mother" reawakens primitive infantile feelings of good object–bad object, omnipotence, and rage—feelings rooted in an early period that predates gender identification of self or object. These archaic remnants, insidiously reinforced by social attitudes, folklore, and the professional literature, contaminate the treatment situation and influence the expectations of both therapists and mother-clients.

MOTHER NEEDS AND THERAPIST EXPECTATIONS

Gluck et al. (1980), in discussing changes in the lives of women during recent years, note that even today more women than men seek therapy either for themselves, their marriages, or their children. They are the "barometers of family tensions and anxieties" (p. 296). These women are mothers seen in a variety of therapeutic contexts. Some are women who enter psychotherapy because of depression, or marital, physical, or economic difficulties; they may feel they are stagnating, are useless, or suffer from what has come to be called the empty nest syndrome. They may have young children and feel guilty because they perceive themselves as inadequate mothers, or because they are bored and would rather not be just a mother. Some are not sure they want to be mothers at all. Some wish, for change but are afraid to make changes in their lives; they may be struggling with a variety of social and/or personal problems. They vary in their coping and adaptability, and in degree of disturbance. Sooner than later they will talk about their children, whether young or grown up. They may ask for advice, or express concern or helplessness; they will be worried about, and often be angry at a child's behaviors. Invariably they will struggle with their view of the acceptable mother, try to conform, and repress or deny any deviation from their version of the ideal. It is not difficult for therapists to understand and to assist verbalization, catharsis, and change, *unless* the wishes and impulses are overwhelmingly negative and threaten the child's well-being.

Yet these situations are relatively benign compared with those in which mothers are involved because their children *are* in therapy. In some of these cases, parents are not seen as clients, with the focus remaining primarily on the needs and treatment of the child. This may occur where there is a disability of one kind or another, and often if the child is in psychoanalysis and in some types of child psychotherapy. In these cases there usually is the belief that the parent, most often the mother, can and will be objective and helpful if told about and educated to the needs of the child. Actually this seemingly positive view may mask a belief in the existence of the ideal mother, whose cooperation is needed and easily and naturally obtained by clarification, intellectualization, and education. For example, mothers will be enlightened about the diagnosis of their children—such as minimal cerebral dysfunction (minimal brain damage), retardation, emotional disturbance, autism, or schizophrenia. Sometimes there is no diagnosis, but some general statements. Most are bad news for parents, some of whom will deny or defend against knowing. Some will become passive or depressed, and others will be angry at the professional. Of course these are not the ways good mothers should act. They are expected to listen, understand, and cooperate in the best interests of the child.

Mothers are frequently given advice. Though most professionals recognize that children's problems may make tremendous demands upon the patience and needs of the whole family, and especially upon the mother, the best interests of the child require that a good mother will implement, at any cost, the helpful suggestions of the professional.

MOTHERS, FATHERS, AND FAMILY ASSESSMENT

With today's focus upon systems and increased recognition of the effect of family interactions on children, we would like to believe that fewer children are in treatment without the involvement of both their parents. Yet the emphasis in most settings still continues to be on the mother. A recent study of parent characteristics in a mental health clinic for young children concluded that no satisfactory analysis could be made because there was a glaring lack of appropriate therapeutic attention to both parents. Interventions were almost exclusively with mothers, training them as teachers of their children, teaching them how to use behavior modification, or offering them a group for mutual support and discussion of such responsibilities as toilet training or discipline (Naylor, 1980).

When there is an assessment of both parents, mothers appear to be more "lethal." They have been called overprotective (Levy, 1970), rejecting (A. Freud, 1970), schizophrenogenic (Fromm-Reichmann, 1948), symbiotically tied (Mahler, 1952; Hill, 1955). Early family therapists attempted to widen the study to include family interactions. Thus Lidz and Lidz (1949), agreeing that fathers may have as noxious an influence as mothers, also concluded that had the fathers been more stable, the potentially schizophrenic child might not have become so embroiled in the pathological symbiosis with the mother. Fathers are described as undercutting their wives' authority, as being hostile and seductive toward their daughters, and as unreasonable in their demands (Lidz et al., 1957). The double-bind situation (Bateson et al., 1956) involves an anxious, hostile mother, who reacts by being too loving toward the child, coupled with the absence of a strong, insightful father to support the child. Fathers have been called distant (Cheek, 1970), passive and ineffectual (Heilbrun, 1973), or defeated, autocratic, oscillating, and chaotic (Jackson et al., 1958). But mothers have been described as manipulating and machiavellian (Jackson et al., 1958).

Chesler (1972) notes:

> Clinician-theorists share the idea that women need to be mothers and that children need intensive and exclusive female mothering in order for both to be mentally "healthy." The absoluteness of this conviction is only equalled by the conviction that mothers are generally "unhappy" and inefficient, and are also the cause of neurosis, psychosis, and criminality in their children. (p. 720)

Mental health clinics, family agencies, and child guidance clinics seem to have a predominance of dominant, aggressive mothers and passive, weak, ineffectual fathers, even when the children are not diagnosed as "schizophrenic." It is as if the helping professions confuse female maturity with dependence and docility and male maturity with dominance (Seidenberg, 1979). In addition mothers who are demanding, who make too many requests of their therapists, or who tell them what to do about their children or other members of the family are frequently considered not amenable to help; they are avoided, rejected, or treated as if they were repulsive (Lieberman & Gottesfeld, 1973).

Spira (1982) has discussed this problem. She notes that one of her roles in her agency was to work with mothers of children in psychotherapy and to focus on the parent–child relationship without excluding other concerns presented by the mothers. With great candor, Spira shared the following:

> There were problems for me in feeling able to meet both my personal standards and the expectation of my position vis-a-vis the mothers. For example, at times I felt an internal pressure to help

a mother become more responsive to the needs of her child beyond her own developmental capacity. My concern about the exacerbation of possible developmental lesions in the child occasionally caused me to empathize more with the child, whom I would attempt to rescue through the mother. . . . My experience and that of other social workers indicate that it is difficult to be helpful to mothers. It occurred to me, however, that a mother's frustrations as a parent, which reopen for her her frustrations as a child, are likely to resonate with the social worker's frustrations in the "nurturing" worker role. As clinicians we might experience more strain in our work with mothers than with other clients. (p. 245)

Mothers frustrate workers just as children frustrate mothers. Is it also possible that frustrated workers have reopened for them their frustrations as children? The child is frustrated at not retaining an imaginary omnipotence; professionals and mothers are frustrated at not achieving this illusory state. Children blame mothers. Mothers blame children and their own mothers, and professionals blame mothers.

THE WICKED WITCH IN LIFE AND LITERATURE

Though developmental growth (abetted by therapy) may enable the relinquishing of dreams of omnipotence, both personally and professionally, and the achievement of fusion of the split-object representations into one not-so-good, not-so-bad, constant object, memory traces of dichotomized very, very good and the very, very bad mother continue to exist. "If psychology has taught us enything, it is the impossibility of exorcising the experience and attitudes of early childhood from our adult frames of reference" (Balfe, 1979, pp. 61–62).

Winnicott (1975) suggests:

A recognition of the absolute dependence of the mother and of her capacity for primary maternal preoccupation, or whatever it is called, is something which belongs to *extreme sophistication* and to a stage not always reached by adults. The general failure of recognition of absolute dependence at the start contributes to the fear of WOMAN that is the lot of both men and women. (p. 304)

In a similar vein, Chesler (1972) says: "Today the world of the spirits is located in our own backyards, or in our own childhoods. Women have "power" not because they are Satan's agents, but because the psychiatrist's mother was a woman—

and she had (and still has) "power" over him" (p. 194). (We should add that she still has power over *her*.)

The powerful place given to women in myth and literature supports this. After all what is myth but a projection of infantile fantasies and wishes (Barglow & Schaefer, 1977). But myths and fairy tales are not written by children; they are written by adults. These commonly present a dual view of woman, as the omnipotent mother goddess who heals, renews, absolves, and offers life, and as a bitch-witch, the evil stepmother or the castrating female.

The witch, the most familiar negative role of the bad mother, has a feared and dangerous magic; the fairy godmother has a wished-for magic. From the child's view, the mother's power to give or withhold comfort seems magical; it is experienced long before it can be understood, antedating language and logic, and in a time when things happen magically. Thus the witch and the good fairy retain the magical power of a woman who can effect these mysterious changes. Every child is frustrated by its mother, no matter how good she tries to be. After all what is really desired is omnipotence. Thus every thwarted child—that is, every child—has a glimpse of the witch behind the beloved face of the mother (Janeway, 1971).

Bettelheim (1976) notes that the figures in fairy tales are never ambivalent. Polarization dominates the child's mind and dominates fairy tales. Thus a person is either good or bad. Bettelheim suggests that the witch, the fairy, and the sorcerer are a reincarnation of the all-good mother of infancy and the all-bad mother of the oedipal crisis, viewed unrealistically as either superhumanly rewarding or inhumanly destructive. In fairy tales the hero, lost in the forest, meets an irresistably attractive witch who satisfies all of his desires. When the hero refuses to do her bidding, she turns against him, changing him into an animal or a stone, or some other nonhuman being.

This scenario occurs long before the oedipal crisis. It suggests the all-satisfying symbiotic relationship as contrasted to the distance and the no's that occur with the child's increasing differentiation, separation, and assertion. Thus, when mother is no longer willing to meet all demands, no matter how unrealistic they are, she is experienced as abandoning, unloving, selfish, and rejecting.

Bloch (1978) says that children's fantasies abound with terrifying beasts, cruel witches, and monsters who threaten to kill them. This fear of infanticide is a consequence of the child's smallness, defenselessness, and helplessness, and the intensity of the fear will reflect the incidence of traumatic events and the degree of violence and of love experienced. The displacement of fears onto monsters and imaginary creatures preserves the idealized image of the parent.

Bettelheim (1976) explains why fairy tales depict fathers as shadowy and ineffectual:

> In the typical nuclear family setting, it is the father's duty to protect the child against the dangers of the outside world, and also those that originate in the child's own asocial tendencies. The mother is to provide nurturing care and the general satisfaction of the immediate bodily needs required for the child's survival. . . . If the mother fails the child . . . the child's very life is in jeopardy. . . . If the father out of weakness is negligent in meeting his obligations, then the child's life as such is not so directly endangered, although a child deprived of the father's protection must shift for himself as best he can. (p. 206)

Janeway (1971) suggests that the myth of female power reflects the early history of human society, when the power of the female seemed awesome because there was no understanding of the part the father played; the mother's impregnation was more easily attributed to the wind, the dew, or an ancestral spirit than to the man with whom she lived. In addition the effective memory of the mother's power over the child is in reality as complete as the child imagines its power over its mother to be.

In a similar vein, Anais Nin (1976, p. 53) reminds us: "If a person continues to see only giants, it means he is still looking at the world through the eyes of a child. I have a feeling that man's fear of woman comes from having first seen her as the mother, creator of men."

PSYCHOLOGY, MAGIC, AND MOTHERS . . . AND FATHERS

The magical power of mothers is reinforced in the professional literature. From Winnicott (1965) we hear that a mother is expected to act by instinct. Though she does not have to have an intellectual understanding of her child's needs, she has to achieve a high degree of identification with them. Though Spitz (1965) enumerates a number of gigantic tasks for mothers, he concludes that the manner in which a good mother divines the needs of her baby is near clairvoyancy, that is to say, magic.

This sets mothers apart from the rest of society where others are taught the basic rules of the jobs they have to do. It is as if women are believed to operate on a more primitive level than is normal for the rest of the world (Janeway, 1971).

Janeway sums it up:

> We must conclude that our society today is asking women to bring off something of an emotional *tour de force*. First, they are asked to regard the bearing and raising of children as at least a very large and significant concern of their lives, and, perhaps, as the crown and center of their existence although, in the nature of things, this undertaking will demand their full efforts for something less than two decades out of a life that will run to seventy years. Second, they must fit their children for a society whose needs and aims are at best uncertain, and which may in fact seem to the mothers as well as the children morally unjustified and emotionally unsatisfying. Third, they are expected to do all this *only* by means of an emotional relationship, instead (as in the past) with the help of economic activities and social processes that relate to the larger world. . . . Fourth, having called forth this relationship, mothers are aware that they should maintain it in such a delicate balance that the child can grow out of it without harm to his own psychic strength. This program they are supposed to carry through with little training and little support from society itself, in the belief that any failure will justly be laid at their door. (p. 162)

Less magic is accorded the father who is usually given a more peripheral role in the caring of children and who is blamed less for the children's problems. His role is rooted in social reality. Winnicott (1965) says the father "supported by a social attitude which is iself a development from man's natural function, deals with the external reality for the woman and so makes it safe and sensible for her to be temporarily in-turned, self-centered" (p. 147). The first and most important virtue for the father is to permit his wife to be a good mother. Yet Winnicott says mothers are responsible for fathers being good fathers, and for whether they do or do not get to know their babies. He also describes the functions of the father as embodying the law, strength, the ideal, and the outside world, while the mother symbolizes the home and the household (Winnicott, 1957). This opinion was echoed more recently by Parens and Saul (1971), who state that the mother provides care taking and indulgence while the father sets limits.

It is only recently that the father's role in the child's early development is coming to be examined with some precision and some parallel to that of the mother (Stewart, 1981; Abelin, 1980; Ross, 1979). Yet his role continues to be an auxiliary one; he is now said to help extricate the child from the maternal orbit, and to facilitate a sense of reality, self-constancy, sexual identity, and other epigenetic achievements that secure object constancy and self-identity (Ross, 1979).

OF OMNIPOTENCE AND RAGE

It was Young (1965) who noted that:

> Parents of course—since they are people after all—often believe in this magic, too. That leaves Mr. and Mrs. John Smith to explain to themselves just why everything hasn't turned out to be precisely the way it was supposed to be. The explanations are apt to be on the feeble side, because magic isn't one of the things you can explain. Mr. and Mrs. Smith usually settle for pretending everything is wonderful and tucking their doubts between the pages of the latest how-to-do-it manual. (p. 9)

Manuals on child care have been best sellers for years, the advice changing from one extreme to another. These are read more by Mrs. Smith than Mr. Smith. What she is really looking for is that magic that will teach her how to attain the status of the ideal mother. She is conditioned by society in its demands upon her, and her own inner demands, her ego ideal, to struggle for omnipotence and perfection in her role as mother.

Edward and colleagues (1981) suggest that the ego ideal is dependent upon the early mother–infant symbiotic experience; it is drawn from this reservoir of early narcissism and omnipotence. This is the stage of the self-mother omnipotence, developed from a beginning dim awareness of an outside source of gratification. Of a later stage, Spitz (1965) notes:

> As long as the child is convinced that he can and does change the world around through omnipotence of thought, he will believe that everybody else can do the same. . . . At this age every grownup is a magician, because the child himself is a magician, even though not quite as successful a magician as the grownup. (p. 113)

In addition children need to believe that their important objects are omnipotent, because only then are the child and the objects safe. This is the childish residue that mothers bring to mothering, a conception magically and unconsciously perceived. It is a residue that therapists also bring to their nurturing role.

But omnipotence is an illusion, unattainable for child, parent, and therapist. The child's earliest fantasies are impinged upon by the reality of the mother and by reality itself. Freud (1911) noted that lack of satisfaction in hallucinating the breast turns the child to the reality of the external world and to the mother. But omnipotence is not relinquished so easily. Spitz (1965, p. 185) talks of "the affective charge of unpleasure" that accompanies frustration; Blanck and Blanck (1979) speak of the infant's organismic distress and Mahler (1952) of affectomotor storm reaction to describe the disturbance of the ungratified infant.

Reality in the form of the child, the simultaneous demands of the larger social world, and the father thwart the mother in her quest for omnipotent mothering. This impotence reawakens earlier memories of childish impotence and stirs childish rage, which, though most often repressed and denied, will be reacted to. To hate a child, and to hate enough to want to kill the child, is rarely admitted, and can only be met with revulsion, by the mother as well as others.

Until recently it was difficult to accept that parents might want to kill their children, that some actually attempt to do so, and that this is a historic fact true of societies in many eras (Bloch, 1978; de Mause, 1974). Bloch (1978), addressing the difficulty of accepting a child's fear of infanticide and a parent's wish to kill the child, reminds us that Freud omitted to discuss the conspiracy of the parents to do away with Oedipus:

> Had Freud applied the same principle of inevitability to the entire myth, his theory would have established the link between cause and effect; the parents' wish to kill their child would then have been universalized as the inevitable first step in the Oedipus complex and as the precipitating factor in the child's preoccupation with incest and murder. (p. 9)

We have become accustomed to hearing clients complain about parents, and to their expressing hateful wishes. But it is still difficult to hear the same sentiments expressed about a child. It is worse when these angry feelings are acted out in abuse and mistreatment of the child. As a result working with abusing parents is difficult and demanding. It is most taxing of therapeutic skill to work with mothers who think like witches, and even more so with those who act like them.

A Mother Who Said: I Wish She Were Dead."

This case example is not extraordinary. The outcome did not meet my fantasies; I performed no miracles.

> Mrs. Morris, a woman in her early 50s, was self-referred. She was a college graduate, married, and in comfortable economic and social circumstances. She was the mother of three children, only one of whom, the youngest at age 17, was living at home. Mrs. Morris said she was unhappy, felt at loose ends, was unfulfilled, and did not know what to do with her life. She said she wanted something for herself.
>
> She spoke rapidly, and almost compulsively. Her physical movements, her thoughts, and all her activities tended to be quick. She said that her young daughter was very difficult, and had been so since she was three. The child had been in psychotherapy since she was six years of age. Then Mrs. Morris asked if the therapist knew anything about schizophrenia. She said she had a lot of documents about her daughter and extended a manila folder, saying, "You can read about her."
>
> She was asked to tell the story as she understood it. She did not know why she had this trouble. Everything had gone wrong when her daughter was three, but she had tried to manage. Then when the child started school, she was advised to get help, and the school referred her to a child psychiatrist. This contact

continued until her daughter was 11, when she was discharged. In early adolescence there was a breakdown that led to hospitalization.

Mrs. Morris talked of contacts with a series of professionals, of intermittent hospitalizations of her daughter, of sending her to a special school. She was asked what the family's involvement had been. She said: "I saw all of them; my husband was seen once." She had regular meetings with the first psychiatrist, about once a month, sometimes more often. "We always talked about my daughter, what the difficulties were, and how I could help her." She said, almost wistfully: "They never saw me for myself. That's why I am here now."

Mrs. Morris was on time for her next appointment, but I was almost an hour late, having made an error about the scheduled time. (I must admit that I engaged myself in serious examination of this mistake, considered various explanations, including that it was related to a repetition of the previous neglect this client seemed to have experienced.)

Mrs. Morris, who had waited, began by suggesting that I had been delayed because of traffic. When asked why she thought so, the client said she had assumed I had been driving, and this could happen. She was asked why she assumed I had been driving. "Of course," she replied, "the train must have been late."

I thanked Mrs. Morris for being such a satisfying client. She was the best I had ever seen. She not only had waited almost an hour without complaining, but she also gave me all the reasons to get off the hook. I said I had not met many people who were so obliging.

She replied: "To tell the truth, I didn't like waiting, but it can happen." I agreed that it had happened, but wondered whether she had wondered, about why it had happened to her. Then we began to talk about her life.

The details of her life were not extraordinary. She talked about her mother, presently confined to a nursing home, whom she visited on a regular basis. She talked about her guilt about not having her mother live with her, but she said she was not an easy woman to live with. Controlling and demanding, she had high standards. Yet her mother had provided special opportunities in the way of schooling and recreation even though the family was poor. Mrs. Morris recalled her childhood as happy; she was always very active, engaged in sports, school, where she did well, and extracurricular activities. Sometimes, she now thought, she was running, and was away from home as much as possible. She liked her father, but he was weak, ill, and unsuccessful; their family had less money and less status than the rest of her mother's family.

As she reviewed her life, she began to express some of her anger at her mother's control, and talked about her own compliance. In describing relationships with others—friends, relatives, and husband—it seemed as if she were a friend in need, supportive, helping, and caring. She was very good, but she was not really easy-going. She had a regularity, a compulsivity, and some rigidity in her relationships and affect. It took time until her resentment at her own unmet needs could be expressed, until she understood the meaning of control to her, and until she could learn to ask to have her needs met.

There were constant detours into discussions about her children. Her model of mothering was to be like her mother, but not like her. On the one hand, she believed that she needed to do everything perfectly for her children, which is how she felt her mother had been. Thus she forced herself to handle everything. At the same time, she tried to be less controlling in the demands she made of her children, and how she monitored their lives.

She talked most about the child who was at home and her helplessness and despair. There had been unpredictable rages directed toward Mrs. Morris, unreasonable, expensive long-distance telephone calls to friends, and soda bottles, dirty dishes, and cigarette ashes littering the house. There were failures to take her medication combined with use of illicit drugs. There were problems with neighbors, and involvement of the police. She complained that when she tried to talk about this to her daughter's psychiatrist, she did not think he understood.

One day, in the midst of this kind of complaining, she said in a quiet but venomous, "I wish she were dead." She went on defiantly, "I know, a mother is not supposed to think this way. But I am overwhelmed." She cried. She talked of how much better off her life would be without her daughter.

I withdrew into myself temporarily to understand.

I knew the daughter was really a trial. But why, when she said she wanted to kill her daughter, did I feel a stab in my heart? Had not the aim of treatment been to release this festering rage? Who was being killed? I reflected that I had fantasies of saving this child whom I did not see, of undoing all the harm that had befallen her. I wondered what made me such an expert that I could do what others had failed to do.

I told Mrs. Morris that the trouble was that she was too good a mother. She disputed this and spoke more of her impatience, her anger. As her death wishes were heard without fear, she became less afraid. As they were accepted as normal, she was able to cry and to mourn the loss of her fantasies of how life could have been, and how her daughter might have been. She talked of what she have liked to have been able to do to control and secure her child's destiny. Nothing she wished was pathological.

As we began to work on how she could be more successful, in limited ways, a different scenario was played out at home. Rules were made and enforced about cleaning up, telephoning, waking, sleeping, money, food, and behavior. There were a few meetings with the father, at Mrs. Morris' request. There were two family meetings in relation to her daughter's request to the mother; the daughter wanted to meet the therapist who had helped her mother become more loving and more helpful.

In the long run, more realistic treatment plans were arranged for the child. Mrs. Morris found resources in a barren area, treatment facilities for the over 18 but not yet adult individual. The daughter was still suffering with a schizophrenic disorder, but her life, and that of her family, was more ordered, and more planned, and therefore more hopeful.

Was Mrs. Morris the rejecting mother? The overprotective mother? The schizophrenogenic mother? She was a woman who expected more from herself than was realistic. This, incidentally, was played out in all areas of her life. As a result she never met her expectations; she always felt a failure; she was always frustrated and always afraid of her rage. In a vicious cycle, she felt even more frustrated about her unacceptable, unacknowledged feelings, and increasingly helpless.

TREATMENT IMPLICATIONS

The first step in working with mothers is for the therapist to work with her or himself. If the nurturing role of the therapist mirrors the nurturing role of the mother, then therapists might have unconscious goals of perfection and omnipotence. Unless these are relinquished and more appropriate aims substituted, the mother with whom the therapist works is in danger; she will be the recipient of antitherapeutic, countertransferential activities. But the wish for omnipotence must be acknowledged. After all what do therapeutic personnel want that is so bad? What we want is only for the client's benefit. If this seems to mirror a mother's statement, it does. What do mothers want but what they perceive as ideal for their children?

The second step is to recognize the affect that accompanies the frustration of therapists who cannot get mothers to do what the therapists know is good for them and, as important, for their children. These affects may be less available to conscious awareness, and because of that, powerful. Only when therapists feel their own affect can they help mothers to cry and rage at being impotent.

The third step is to establish realistic goals for the therapeutic endeavor, to change aims in the interest of reality and coping. Then therapists will be more successful in helping mothers to help their children more realistically.

CONCLUSIONS

I have suggested that the difficulties therapists experience in working with mothers are similar to the difficulties mothers have in being mothers. Mothers expect to be omnipotent because of internal and external pressures. When this is thwarted by the child and the mother is impotent, the rage that results is reflective of childish experiences. This will be expressed, repressed, and experienced differently, depending upon the mother's level of development and the nature of her life's experience.

Therapists expect to be omnipotent because of internal and external pressures. When this is thwarted by the mother and the therapist feels impotent, the rage that results is also reflective of childish experiences. This will be expressed, repressed, and experienced differently, depending upon the therapist's self-awareness and professional knowledge and skill.

For both therapist and mother, the impotence of the mother and self reawakens an early rage at one's own mother's fallibility. This is why being a mother and working with mothers are more complicated than any other kind of work.

It has been said that Mother's Day is society's rite of atonement (Spiegel, 1971). It is appropriate that the social work profession, the one that works with more mothers than any other, pay tribute to all our struggling mother-clients, past and present. It is appropriate that we say: "Mothers, forgive us our trespasses, for we do not always know what we do."

REFERENCES

Abelin, E. L. 1980. Triangulation, the role of the father and the origins of care gender identity during the rapprochement subphase. In *Rapprochement: The critical subphase of separation-individuation*, R. F. Lax, S. Bach, and J. A. Burland (Eds.). New York: Jason Aronson.

Balfe. J. H. 1979. Shame, guilt and the development of mariolatry. In *Psychosexual imperatives*, M. C. Nelson and J. Ikenberry (Eds.). New York: Human Sciences Press.

Barglow, P. , and M. Schaefer. 1977. A new female psychology? In *Female psychology: Contemporary psychoanalytic views*, H. P. Blum (Ed.). New York: International Universities Press.

Bateson, G., D. D. Jackson, J. Haley, and J. H. Weakland. 1956. Toward a theory of schizophrenia. *Behav. Sci.* 1:251–264.

Bettelheim, B. 1976. *The uses of enchantment.* New York: Alfred A. Knopf.

Blanck, G., and R. Blanck. 1979. *Ego psychology II.* New York: Columbia University Press.

Bloch, D. 1978. *So the witch won't eat me.* Boston: Houghton-Mifflin. Boston Women's Health Book Collective.

———. 1971. *Our bodies, ourselves.* New York: Simon & Schuster.

Cheek, F. E. 1970. The schizophrenogenic mother in word and deed. In *Family process*, N. Ackerman (Ed.). New York: Basic Books.

Chesler, P. 1972. *Women and madness.* New York: Doubleday.

de Mause, L. (Ed.). 1974. *The history of childhood.* New York: Psycho History Press.

Edward, J., N. Ruskin, and P. Turrini. 1981. *Separation-individuation: Theory and application.* New York: Gardner Press.

Freud, A. 1970. The concept of the rejecting mother. In *Parenthood. Its psychology and psychopathology*, E. J. Anthony and T. Benedek (Eds.). Boston: Little, Brown.

Freud, S. 1911. Formulations regarding the two principles in mental functioning. In *Collected Papers* Vol. 4, E. Jones (Ed.). New York: Basic Books, 1955.

Fromm-Reichmann, F. 1948. Notes on the development of schizophrenia by psychoanalytic psychotherapy. *Psychiatry* 267–277.

Gluck, N. R., E. Dannefer, and K. Milea. 1980. Women in families. In *The family life cycle: A framework for family therapy*, E. A. Carter and M. McGoldrick (Eds.). New York: Gardner Press.

Heilbrun, A. B. 1973. *Aversive maternal control: A theory of schizophrenic development.* New York: John Wiley & Sons.

Hill, L. B. 1955. *Psychotherapeutic intervention in schizophrenia.* Chicago: University of Chicago Press.

Jackson, D. D., J. Block, and V. Patterson. 1958. Psychiatrists' conceptions of the schizophrenic parents. *Arch. of Neurol. Psychiatry* 79:448–459.

Janeway, E. 1971. *Man's world, woman's place: A study in social mythology.* New York: William Morrow.

Levy, D. M. 1970. The concept of maternal overprotection. In *Parenthood. Its psychology and psychopathology*, E. J. Anthony and T. Benedek (Eds.). Boston: Little, Brown.

Lidz, R. W. and T. Lidz. 1948. The family environment of schizophrenic patients. *Am. J. Psychiatry* 106:332–345.

Lidz, T., A. Corneleson, S. Sleck, and D. Terry. 1957. Intrafamilial environment of the schizophrenic patient. I: The father. *Psychiatry* 20:329–342.

Lieberman, F., and M. L. Gottesfeld. 1973. The repulsive client. *Clin. Soc. Work J.* 1:22–31.

Mahler, M. S. 1952. On childhood psychosis and schizophrenia: Autistic and symbiotic infantile psychosis. In *Psychoanalytic Study of the Child*, Vol. VII. New York: International Universities Press, pp. 286–305.

Naylor, A. K. 1980. Early intervention: Panacea or challenge? Characteristics of parents in a mental health clinic for young children. In *The child in his family: Preventive child psychiatry in an age of transition*, Vol. 6, E. J. Anthony and C. Chiland (Eds.). New York: John Wiley & Sons.

Nin, A. 1966. *Diary, 1931–1934*. New York: Swallon Press, Harcourt, Brace & World.

Parens, H., and L. J. Saul. 1971. *Dependence in man*. New York: International Universities Press.

Ross, J. M. 1979. The forgotten father. In *Psychosocial imperatives*, M. C. Nelson and J. Ekenberry (Eds.). New York: Human Sciences Press.

Seidenberg, R. 1979. Psychoanalysis and the femininst movement. In *Psychosexual imperatives* M. C. Nelson and Ikenberry (Eds.). New York: Human Sciences Press.

Spiegel, John. 1971. *Transactions: The interplay between individual, family and society*. New York: Science House.

Spira, J. 1982. Professional development: The client's contribution. *Soc. Casework.* 63:244–246.

Spitz, R. A. 1965. *The first year of life*. New York: International Universities Press.

Stewart, J. M. 1981. The second dyad. In *Smith College studies in social work*, Lll.

Winnicott, D. H. 1957. *The Child and the family: First relationships*. London; Robestock.

————. 1965. *The maturational processes and the facilitating environment*. New York: International Universities Press.

————. 1975. *Through pediatrics to psycho-analysis*. New York: Basic Books.

Young, L. 1965. *Life among the giants*. New York: McGraw-Hill.

DISCUSSION

Lucille Spira

Florence Lieberman reminds us that all of us—practitioners, mothers, and children—still long for unfulfilled childhood fantasies of omnipotence. She well describes the transgressions against the mother-client that can result when this universal wish for omnipotence is transformed into an expectation. Those of us engaged as mental health professionals will do well to reflect on Lieberman's thesis and its practice implications.

Her concerns add to our understanding of why mothers who are in the patient role pose special challenges for therapists. This discussion proceeds from the perspective that an examination by therapists and mental health professionals of their role vis-à-vis the mother-client is mandatory.

The idea that therapists aggress against those mothers who have a child in treatment because of the therapists' own grandiose expectations, and the inevitable sense of impotence that is bound to result where these unrealistic expectations exist, has ramifications both for our work with mothers and for our professional development. Lieberman suggests that therapists who treat mothers need to accept their own lack of omnipotence, because it is only then that the therapist can serve as a more benign superego introject to the mother-client. In turn this can help the patient to develop more realistic expectations of self and object.

The Morris case, poignantly described, sharpens our sensitivity to the plight of the mother-client as it highlights the effect of a mother's struggle with herself, her child, and the mental health establishment where negative attitudes toward mothers with disturbed children can prevail. The case also illustrates the complexity of the dynamics that occur in work with such mothers, particularly as we look at the didactic and experiential aspects of the treatment skillfully undertaken by Lieberman.

Elkisch (1953), restating Kestenberg, reminds us that by definition a parent whose child needs psychotherapy suffers a narcissistic injury. Mrs. Morris' depression and anger support this idea. Although Lieberman believes that patients like Mrs. Morris are treated unfairly by therapists, such mothers, may, in fact, receive more empathy than many others who will be described later in this discussion.

Mrs. Morris' defensive repertoire is one in which her aggression, at least overtly, is primarily directed against herself. Although she has aggressive thoughts about her daughter, they might be rationalized away because the daughter appears to be an impulsive adolescent who could be considered by some to be more of a victimizer than a victim. Most important, Mrs. Morris does not directly discharge her aggression toward the therapist; and this could lead therapists to experience her more neutrally.

Social workers, and perhaps other psychotherapy professionals, are likely to feel more inadequate when a patient's anger is directed toward them (Spira, 1984). Therefore, while mental health practitioners should consider Lieberman's thesis as they engage with clients who are mothers, they should especially consider it when the client is one who readily directs her aggression toward the therapist. It is this client rather than ones like Mrs. Morris who seem most likely to be characterized as repulsive and reacted to as such.

STRAINS ON THE WORKER

Selma Fraiberg and her co-workers (1975) describe mothers who appear to be very different from Mrs. Morris and who are likely to challenge even the most mature therapist. Fraiberg's mothers are young women whose infants are at risk not only for emotional deprivation but for infanticide. These mothers, because of internal conflicts partly rooted in experiences with sadistic objects, engage in what could be life-threatening sadistic practices with their young children. It is Fraiberg's contention that such mothers reenact their own traumas with their children and can be directly aggressive toward their therapists who seem to be viewed as persecutors and intruders.

It seems important to note that there are mothers who by virtue of the way in which their internal world is organized cannot connect, even in the most basic way, with their infant. These mothers seem best described as suffering from failures to perceive reality rather than from failures to live up to unreachable ideals resulting from fantasies of omnipotence or wishes to be the ideal mother. Social workers sometimes at the outset of their careers are confronted by mothers whose situations require knowledge and skill beyond the practitioner's level of development. The effect that situations such as the ones described by Fraiberg have on the way social workers come to regard the mother-client is not addressed by Lieberman. The stance of the supervisor toward the worker and the tendency to promote the worker's omnipotence fantasies also is not discussed, although it seems an important implication of Lieberman's concern. Lieberman's emphasis is the danger inherent in allowing a fantasy of future omnipotence to persist. Therapists and supervisors, as we follow Lieberman, should proceed with caution where this occurs, because there are situations in which infantile aims are most at risk to be pursued, with opportunities lost for real self-enhancement.

Lieberman is not alone in her interest in mothers as individuals and as clients. Although she does not discuss efforts on the part of practitioners to address the needs of mothers sensitively, there are programs that have this as an aim.

The "Mother's Center," as Turrini (1977) refers to her program, is one that utilizes psychoanalytic theory and aims to avert trauma to the self-esteem of mothers while it attempts to augment and develop services for them. The program proceeds from the idea that the mothers' own experiences give them something valuable to share with others. Therefore, a major focus is the work done by the mothers who meet in groups designed to address particular needs and interests appropriate to the mother's personal situation. The idea is that the atmosphere and group process, combined with the filtering of support and information, can enhance self-esteem. At the center, according to Turrini, perceptions about children and motherhood can be refined and distortions and inappropriate expectations can be revised in a nonjudgmental and supportive atmosphere.

A program with the thrust to protect and build the self-esteem of mothers can only occur as we understand Lieberman's ideas, where the professional staff members are able to control their own fantasies of omnipotence and have established realistic self-perceptions. The idea can be entertained that had Mrs. Morris, many years earlier, been exposed to professionals who had internalized the philosophy of Benedek, Fraiberg, Turrini, and Lieberman, she would have experienced herself and her child in a more integrated way. Mrs. Morris and her daughter might still have needed treatment, but one could hypothesize that Mrs. Morris might have been able to approach her treatment from a position of strength instead of demoralization.

In summary, Lieberman has contributed to our understanding of the complexities involved in work with mothers. She alerts mental health professionals engaged in work with mothers to be acutely aware of their own countertransference, because, as she sees it, omnipotence fantasies that belong to childhood are at risk to be acted upon. Supportive supervision and the worker's exposure to less pejorative programs that sensitively address the needs of mothers may also help the clinician to be more effective with the mother-client.

REFERENCES (Discussion)

Benedek, T. 1959. Parenthood as a developmental phase: A contribution to the libido theory. *J. Am. Psychoanal. Assoc.* 7:389–417.

Elkisch, P. 1953. Simultaneous treatment of a child and his mother. *Am. J. Psychother.* 7:123.

Fraiberg, S., E. Adelson, and V. Shapiro. 1975. Ghosts in the nursery: A psychoanalytic approach to the problems of the impaired infant–mother relationship. *J. Am. Acad. Child Psychiatry* 14(3):387–421.

Spira, L. 1984. Perceptions of M.S.W. clinicians about agency and private supervision. Unpublished doctoral dissertation, New York University.

Turrini, P. 1977. A mothers' center: Research, services and advocacy. *Soc. Work.* 22(6):478–483.

5 *Further Extensions of Theory and Practice*

Reuben Blanck

The author extends the contributions of Greenacre, Mahler, Spitz, et al. in bringing precision to the term "transference" by showing that the intaking processes in primary dyadic and triadic relationships lead to later transference manifestations. Through an in-depth analysis of the patients' and therapists' process in a treatment dialogue, Blanck demonstrates the application of his theoretical ideas.

DISCUSSION by J. R. Montgomery Montgomery lends clarity to the "ground base" upon which Blanck has expanded theory and its clinical application through a precise conceptualization of the contributions of the psychoanalytic developmentalists to the concept of transference. This expansion of theory and technique is making possible the successful treatment of a less-than-neurotic patient population.

Transference phenomena have their origins in the force field in which the neonate's total dependence—at this point its parasitically shaped libido—interacts with the life-supporting object. My references to the drives are based upon Freud's last statement in 1940, that libido is the force that seeks connections, and strives to create ever-greater unities, and that the aggressive drive serves autonomy by undoing connections and, as we have added, enabling connections to be reestablished on higher levels of psychic structure. Thus the drives are differentiated from affects, libido not being synonymous with love, nor the aggressive drive with hostility. Transference manifestations constitute reflections of levels of object relations. They are patterns that have been laid down in primary object experiences, internalized so that they have become part of the structure. It is useful to consider what the form of structure is, that is, how much internal processing has taken place before structuralization.

To recapitulate briefly, intaking processes have been described as direct, an emotional tie before object cathexis (Freud, 1921); as the coenesthetic reception that Spitz (1965) described as a global affective visceral intaking. They have also

109

been described as the defensive form of identification to obviate object loss (Freud, 1917b); and by Jacobson (1964) as the process of selective identification.

INTERNALIZING GLOBALLY AND BY PSYCHIC STRUCTURE PROCESSING

There are two major ways of internalizing, those that are coenesthetically received in a global way, as described by one of Freud's definitions and by Spitz, and those that have been subjected to processing by a psychic structure. As Spitz (1965) said, in relation to the former, "We are accustomed to thinking of the attributes of the coenesthetic organization in terms of the unconscious. But from the developmental viewpoint, its role in the total economy of the 'system person' is compellingly evident." He stated also, "We shall show that, much as the coenesthetic organization has become muted in the consciousness of Western man, it continues to function covertly; what is more, it plays a momentous determining role in our feelings, our thinking, our actions—even though we try to keep them under wraps" (p. 45). Currently support for the existence of global reflexive intaking processes is provided by the neonatal studies that demonstrate that infants at a very early age can be seen to respond to the mother and others.

In relation to the latter, as the self-images coalesce into self-representations and a measure of constancy of the self-representations is acquired, these begin to effect a gradual reduction in the totality of the scope of the object images. Needless to say, this process also requires that the object representations also acquire constancy, as the infant begins to cope with the enormously anxiety-provoking stage of differentiation. Maturation of physical capacities pushes the process forward and aids the infant's development toward tolerating the inevitable anxiety aroused by the process of increased physical and psychological distancing. Gratification in the exercise of function becomes the tool by which the distancing process—separation-individuation—is furthered and aided by internalization. The processing of input may involve defensive operations, which in turn may or may not change in function and become adaptive. Or they may reflect high-level structural internalizing process, such as selective identification.

CONNECTING TRANSFERENCE AND STRUCTURAL THEORY

Transference has been defined as the reproduction of feelings and attitudes toward a person in the past, displaced upon a person in the present. As such it involves a certain quality of failure in reality testing because current reality is, to some extent, obscured. Also involved is a touch of infantile narcissistic grandiosity, since transference feelings involve "knowing" the attitude of the other person, albeit frequently a misperception.

Psychoanalysis began, historically, with the treatment of the well-structured personality, or at least the attempt was made to restrict the analytic method to those whom it could have a good chance of helping. In such situations it was thought that attitudes, affects, behavior—that is, object relations with a primary object—are transferred in the analytic situation. Although the theory did not at first have matters conceptualized, retrospectively we can apply modern terminolgy and conceptualization to that interesting phenomenon. Now we can see that some of the assumptions about the transference neuroses included prior acquisition of self and object constancy, with relatively clear demarcation of self and object representations, and relatively secure boundaries between the two sets of representations. Those patients fortunately suffering with a transference neurosis could be helped to understand, by means of interpretation in the analytic encounter, that their perception of the analyst—and of the object world—had become biased and distorted by experience of conflict that could not be coped with by the infantile ego. The therapeutic experience in analysis could then become the medium through which such misperceptions could be "worked through" by the presumably more rational and more capable ego of the adult in the subsequent treatment experience.

The less fortunate sufferers with the narcissistic neuroses could not be touched sufficiently by the therapeutic experience—the analyst had little or no effect—and this indicated that their disturbances were of a different order.

With the advent of the structural theory, there could be little doubt that the difference in diagnosis was not so much a difference in the disease but a difference in the structure. This was compellingly formulated by K. Eissler in 1953 when he suggested that the significant factor in pathology was not the structure of the symptom but the structure of the ego in which the symptom was embedded. The capacities for object connection differed vastly, accounting for the differences in availability for restructuring, reorganizing, and "cure." This changed the understanding of the nature of the transference. It is not that in the narcissistic neuroses there was no "transfer"; the difference was that the capacity for object relations in the present—in the treatment—was not of sufficient strength or meaning to enable such individuals to rework, revise, or alter their misperceptions of the object world, and especially to do so with the help of a person in the current object field. One of the one-on-one, obviously the therapist, was not cathected with sufficient clout to gain enough important effect in the current relationship to promote growth.

Our own thoughts on these phenomena went through the following process. We were impressed clinically by the fact that seemingly obvious distortions of reality appeared to such patients as absolute reality. Recognition of this fact led us to attempt to distinguish between neurotic transference phenomena on the one hand and, on the other, the seemingly unanalyzable infantile reactions to primary figures that resulted in a fixed misperception of the object world in the present. Since these misperceptions of the real world unfortunately constituted the experienced perceptions of the primary object world of the past, we tried to distinguish between the need for replication of early object experience and true transference, i.e., displaced, distortions (Blanck & Blanck, 1977). Subsequently (Blanck & Blanck, 1979) coming closer to focusing the problem in the structure itself, we distinguished interpretable transference manifestations from those that could not be interpreted, but that might, to some extent, shift in a sustained experience of a different (that is, more growth-promoting) relationship, including appropriately timed frustration, and we especially distinguished these two from fixed impressions that defy modification or alteration.

What must be stressed here is that transference processes—that is, misperceptions of persons in the current reality—are ubiquitous and are present in the delusions of the psychotic, the uncongenial fantasies of the less-than-structured, as well as the interpretable displaced misperceptions of the "normal neurotic." It is a phenomenon of human development, in that the existence of a human object is an irreplaceable necessity for growth.

The early global reception processes strongly influence acquisition of reality testing. To be accurate one should refer only to perception of reality since human reality testing remains subjective and is modified by the emotional state. The practicing infant can become very upset with the mother, who protectively restrains the child from running out into the heavily trafficked road. But the child's perception of reality is very different from that of the mother, as it is limited to the child's need to exercise the important functions of motility, curiosity, exploration, and gathering of experiences in the object world, and the like. Both perceptions, the toddler's and the mother's, are "correct," although obviously the mother's perception must dominate the toddler's more limited capacity to perceive the whole reality. But limitations on perceptual grasp of reality remain, although, it is hoped, they will diminish throughout life.

OBJECT RELATIONS AND REALITY TESTING

While we tend to think that objective experiences have the major role in the acquisition of reality testing, object relations also play a decisive role. As structure develops, as the child takes over more and more of the functions of the protecting objects, there is greater opportunity to come closer to experiencing the actual "reality" of the world at large, separate and different from the object's perception. Thus each individual's ongoing growth-promoting separating-individuating processes provide the opportunity to develop a grasp of reality closer to the objective state of things, but always short of true objectivity.

The very existence of transference phenomena proves that true objectivity is out of human reach. Every scientific paper proves this idea in the fact that the bibliographical references illuminate the effect that psychological forebears have had upon the writer. Some of them are differed with, some are modified and extended, and there are some whose influence is still paramount. In successful treatment the resolution of the transference neurosis means that a greater capacity for more objective perception and apperception has been achieved, but this remains relative and is far from absolute. In any event we cannot separate from our roots, nor is it desirable to do so.

Thus we come to understand that there are intaking processes of a psychological nature from day one. As psychic structure is built, expands, and integrates, the intaking "material" is more and more subjected to structural processing. The quality of the separation-individuation process constitutes a decisive factor in determining how well input is processed by a functioning system, or to what extent input becomes something to absorb viscerally, unthinkingly, so to speak, or to what extent it is globally resisted. Finally we understand that there is probably a core of ineradicable internalizations that have become fixed assumptions forming character; others can be modified by experience, and there are those that have been selectively internalized by a functioning psychic system that has developed a more flexible capacity to make choices and decisions. This description parallels the distinction between primary and secondary processes in that the latter also denotes the existence of a functioning structure that uses its apparatuses—intelligence, speech, perception, and the like—to deal with reality.

We see that transference is a universal phenomenon containing the residue of early object experiences. Similarly "reality" testing is also conditioned by object relations. Also, object relations in optimal growth situations include structured patterns that begin with global receptivity, and move on to higher and higher levels of structural processing of input as individual structure takes shape and form and is integrated. Finally all levels of internalization exist in each person. The reality each individual is capable of perceiving derives from the extent to which individual identity formation is capable of using the ego's capacities to make adaptive judgments and decisions.

SIGNIFICANCE OF ATTACHMENT IN ORGANIZATION

Flexible attunement to the object world becomes thereby a significant diagnostic criterion. The toddler, who was prevented by the mother from running into a dangerous situation, has suffered a narcissistic injury, and will, or should, reward the mother for her protective effort with a howl of protest and tears. The child may be diverted into a safer activity, but the important aspect of this vignette lies in the ongoing relationship between mother and child. In normal growth the positive balance of experiences, coupled with the necessity for maintaining safety feeling (Sandler, 1960) that derives from maintenance of connection with the object, will outweigh the frustrating ones and thus provide a growth-promoting medium in which omnipotence is gradually discouraged, but normal expansion of opportunity within safe limits is encouraged. This constitutes the optimal experience of frustration so necessary for the gradual reduction of grandiosity and omnipotence specific to the practicing subphase, and also promotes the development of anxiety tolerance.

To the extent that development proceeds normally, the overall organizing capacity can use reality testing and negotiating processes to reduce the impact and scope of the object representations and to enhance and increase the scope of the self representations. Adaptation and fitting together in the current object world constitute the overall goal, one in which both libidinal and aggressive drive needs become harmonized. This cannot produce total harmony, but the direction is toward a state of relative harmony and equilibrium.

With respect to these early impressions, while the ordinary daily life experiences will have brought some necessity for modification of many of them, it cannot be expected that all such early impressions will have come up in ordinary experience for reconsideration and reworking. Some at least remain, retaining their nonnegotiable quality, totally incorporated into character structure. These might be referred to as a precipitate of abandoned object cathexes, except that they are internalized and are far from being abandoned.

APPLYING THEORY TO TREATMENT

Now that we know so much about the less-than-structured patient, questions arise about techniques for treatment. Nowhcrc is this more important than as it relates to the use of transference. It is even correct to say that no other therapeutic tool has value unless it is applied within the context of understanding the nature of that part of the therapeutic relationship that we call transference. Although transference was first used in the more restricted sense described (as transfer), its usage has broadened and it is sometimes applied to all aspects of the therapeutic relationship. Our preference is to distinguish sharply among transference, transference-like phenomena, including replication of early object experience, and the other aspects of the therapeutic relationship such as the therapeutic alliance (Zetzel, 1956) or the working alliance (Greenson, 1965). To so distinguish provides a better approach to clear designation of the level of object relations. If the entire therapeutic field is described as transference, little opportunity exists to examine the precise meaning and manner of approach to the therapist and thereby make an assessment of the level of object relations of which the structure is capable and which directs that approach.

Many questions have arisen as to whether we can apply the same techniques to which we have become accustomed in treating the more highly developed structures to the less developed. This applies particularly to our expectations of the patient's behavior in the transference. A much overlooked discovery made by Jacobson in 1964 was elaborated by us in 1979. Jacobson said, "In adult patients we must not confuse transference processes based on displacement from one object image to another, such as from the mother onto the analyst, with projections" (p. 47).

The distinction drawn here between these two defense mechanisms is significant when examined from a viewpoint that assesses the structural level of functioning in the individual employing these defenses. Displacement involves a processed level of object relations, transferring attitudes and feelings appropriate to object A to object B. Projection, on the other hand, is not all that specifically object related, and requires only the presence, or even the thought, of another for emplacement therein of the subject's own feelings and ideas, rather than the recognition of another separate individual. Reality testing, while inaccurate in both, is nonetheless more globally deficient in projection. In displacement the object of the displacement usually has to do something to trigger the defense, whereas in projection the entire process is intrapsychic and need not involve interpersonal interaction for it to run off.

This suggests that a distinction must be drawn between interpretable transference and the phenomena within the therapeutic field that do not represent displacement from a whole-object representation of the past to the therapist in the present. The object relations levels of the less than fully structured patients vary from one individual to another, and even fluctuate from time to time within the same individual. The long familiar and all-too-global mother transferences or father transferences are not applicable. Negotiation or approaches to the therapist are based on lesser levels of object relations, levels on which there is less differentiation between self and object images, that is, where neither self nor other is experienced as a separate whole person. As object relations determine the style of contact with the therapist, levels can range from regarding the object exclusively as a need gratifier, as part of the self images at varying degrees of self-object differentiation, as one with whom to repeat experiences with the primary object in order to retain a likeness of that object, and thereby to prevent object loss and hence overwhelming anxiety and depression, to the maximum level of negotiations with separate whole representations of another.

Whether transference phenomena can be interpreted in treatment depends upon the level of object relations achieved, disregarding for the moment the differences in therapeutic skill. More specifically, the development of the capacity for interpretable transference—which approximates Freud's concept of the transference neurosis—represents the success of the third organizer of the psyche—semantic communication. This is far more than the simple acquisition of speech, as Spitz (1965) has pointed out. Forms of communication exist long before language can be operative, both phylogenetically and ontogenetically. The question becomes one of determining the extent to which semantic communication has really become an affective and effective modus operandi bewteen self and object. In turn this depends upon the degree to which language has replaced earlier forms of communication in dyadic and triadic experiences. This represents a momentous leap in development, but momentous as it is, it never becomes total and is always subject to regression in profound emotional states.

WORDS AND EXPERIENCE

For a long period words are either unavailing or quite inadequate. The infant and the toddler at about 12 months plus understand far more than they can respond to in words. During this period affective imbalance totally undercuts semantic communication and replaces it with behavioral forms. In adult life we try to convey the same by saying, "I'm at a loss for words." The toddler's serious and intensive study of language can achieve gratifying effects with the primary object or objects, but it also becomes one of the tools for separation-individuation, and therefore, at times, a mixed blessing for the toddler. The primary object uses other means as well as words to convey positive affirming responses to the child, but also must use words to convey prohibitions, frustrations, and negative feelings as well. This most important tool, therefore, is also molded and developed according to the quality and affective balance of primary object experiences. The importance of Jacobson's phrase (1964) "evenly distributed cathexis" needs to be stressed, for it is the existence of a positively balanced cathexis of the object that is crucial to the development of a positively balanced cathexis of the self representations. So, as semantic communication replaces other forms of communication, which includes coenesthetic reception, the quality of the primary relationship becomes an overriding factor in determining how successfully object retention is maintained as identity formation proceeds and semantic communication furthers separation-individuation. It may well have been this factor that led Sullivan to distrust verbal communication, referring to it in the following way, as stated by Mullahy (1970):

Language has not proved to be an unmixed blessing. By verbal behavior man can communicate many sorts of things: things false or fanciful as well as true...Man has been handicapped by witting and unwitting interference with his life by the relatively few who are particularly apt at verbal performances, some of whom exploit their relative advantage in the pursuit of short-sighted personal gain. (p. 120)

Since Sullivan dealt mainly with schizophrenics, their structures would not have been such as to enable them to combine semantic communication with positive affective connection with their objects. The very attempt to get a regressed person to speak unfortunately deals with the symptom instead of with a psychic structure that has found compelling reasons to withdraw from communication with the object world. Obviously it is much easier to induce or seduce a regressed individual into uttering some words than it is to undertake a task so global as to bring the very quality of object relations into therapeutic focus.

Those who have, in Lichtenberg's words (1975), learned to live less in the body and more in the mind, will be found to be more available to interpretations. Those who are still living more in the body—that is, in the experience—and less in the structure depend far more heavily upon the affective tone of the therapeutic relationship, which conveys far greater meaning than words, or interpretations.

This may be far more difficult to assess than appears on the surface. A patient with an extremely low threshold for frustration is prone to becoming very angry and upset with the therapist, and to shout and rage in the session. The patient all too often leaves sessions in such a state. (Once again it is necessary here to leave out the issue of therapeutic skill, although this is obviously very important.) Invariably, however, the patient returns and treatment can be continued. The issue for differential diagnosis here is the all-important question as to whether the rage has been worked through by means of the patient's structural capacity to do just that and renegotiate the matter verbally with the therapist, or whether it is a libidinal need for ongoing connection that makes the patient so fearful of object loss as to be unable to evaluate the situation more appropriately. Anxiety aroused by the latter circumstance may force patients to continue regardless of whether it is really in their best interests.

SAFETY FEELINGS AND DEVELOPMENT

In discussing the acquisition of the capacity for interpretable transference—that is, the transference neurosis—we are discussing a general theory of psychological development. While this is obviously too broad in scope for the present discussion, some abbreviated general outline of its form can be attempted. The maintenance of a feeling of safety in infancy is an absolute; since safety feeling is inexorably a product of connection with the object and later with objects, the drive toward connection and the attainment of a safety feeling are initially identical. This describes symbiosis.

As internal capacities increase as a result of both maturation of physical capacities and development of psychological functions, the aggressive drive comes into ascendancy (Blanck & Blanck, 1979). By aggressive we limit our thinking to the drive to undo connections (Freud, 1940) in order to find and establish individual identity. This engages the differentiating infant and the practicing and rapprochement toddler in a gargantuan endeavor, so well observed and described by Mahler. This struggle must be resolved by postponement of independence and acceptance of the inexorable fact of childhood dependency. This same struggle is repeated during the oedipal crisis. It is only during and after adolescence that the differentiating individuating needs and wishes can come into final ascendance, aided not only by the vastly reduced physical dependency needs and acceptance of the generation gap, but, most important, by the establishment of connection with an object of one's own generation. Adolescence is a period of oscillation between exhilaration and despair precisely because the loosening of infantile connections to the primary family produces sadness and depression, while the prospect or hoped-for reality of new connections on a more independent level becomes exhilarating, in spite of the fact that at this age such connections are usually transient. In this way the need for connection, for libido, is brought into harmony with the drive for independent identity, the aggressive drive. Maintenance of safety feeling has become internalized, that is, it has become the individual's own functional responsibility, which, however, can be sustained only by new connections with new objects. It represents a triumph of both the internalizing processes that have thereby maintained connection with objects, and the drive toward individuation and separate identity. Independence is thus "relatively" achieved.

As must be obvious, there are enormous differences in the shape and form of "normal" acquisition of identity. Beyond that there are myriad opportunities for pathological malformation. To return to the issue of treatment, under the most optimal circumstances the therapist must be able to draw the patient's capacity for object connection into the therapeutic interaction.

This was, of course, discovered in Freud's clinical experience, out of which he was able to conceptualize the idea of a transference neurosis to indicate two facts: first, that the patient had to have the capacity to connect with the therapist, and, second, that the therapist has to find the means to connect with the patient. Out of the former, Freud developed his remarkable theories of psychic development. Out of the latter came his thoughts on technique, especially the papers on technique, on transference, and wild analysis. These reflections convinced him of the necessity for "neutrality," by which we believe he meant absence of value judgment, evenly suspended attention, the careful, noncritical attention to resistance and defense. Neutrality did not mean a totally objective attitude toward the patient, and Freud's attitudes toward his patients cannot be described as uncaring. Especially his response to resistance—"the best support" for treatment and the like—demonstrates Freud's interest in and capacity to go with the patient. As far back as 1895, Freud's response to Elizabeth von R.'s resistance led him "to make a careful note" when this phenomenon occurred.

Therefore the most careful assessment must be made of the level of object relations evident in the transference manifestations to enable the therapist to decide upon the response that has the best therapeutic potential.

TRANSFERENCE FORMS ILLUSTRATED

In the following case example, various forms of transference can be designated as interpretable, not yet interpretable, and fixed assumptions. These all occur in the space of a single hour with one patient. Although this is a long-term patient, the various forms of transference probably occur in the same way in many, if not most, therapeutic hours.

The necessity for the therapist to tolerate uncertainty must also be stressed—not really to know how a person will react until we learn from the patient what effects our interventions have produced. Levels of object relations differ not only among people, but also in the same person from time to time. This will illuminate the intricacies and complexities of working with structure.

One patient's major difficulty is her fear of success, which has led her to fear her functional capacity. An extraordinarily talented woman, she becomes terrified by her own talents and usually manages to leave tasks uncompleted or to finish them in such a crunch that her only recourse is to avoid future tasks. She took something like 12 years to complete her doctoral dissertation, and then only by the barest margin. Her avoidance of function has the purpose of avoiding anticipated disaster or annihilation. Over many years of work, the therapist has been able to help her expand her horizon, including finishing her doctoral dissertation, and so she now does much more than she had done in the past. Her reaction to this helpfulness is an odd admixture—a touch of appreciation thoroughly leavened with anger, which, of course, is the outward expression of her anxiety. This has resulted because the therapist, in her distorted fantasy, has taken her another step toward annihilation. Here we can see the existence of a fixed assumption that reality has not yet overcome. Fortunately for the therapeutic experience, her progress is not based upon compliance, but upon a genuine pursuit of her own interests involving her considerable capacities. Thus she cannot totally blame the therapist for her progress, but has to accept at least part of the blame herself. I am touching briefly here upon the experience of having helped a patient to accomplish a long-term goal only to find her thoroughly unappreciative of that achievement.

Some snatches of the treatment dialogue around the current issue are provided in the following. The patient is an accomplished musician, although that is not her major field. She has studied with teachers who have participated in training first-rank concert artists. Such teachers choose their pupils carefully, so it is clear that the patient is unusually talented.

The discussion concerns a recital for which she is preparing, to be given a few days after the session cited. The work of the preceding weeks consisted of dealing with her usual threats to call off the concert, fire the musical coach, terminate therapy, and kill herself. In the years of therapy, the patient and the therapist have been through this probably a dozen times, but the pattern is invariably the same. There is no carryover from a previous success, only the dreadful fear that she will not know how to play, will lose her place, will fall off the chair or fall into a faint, and similar feeling of disintegration.

Patient: When that happens I feel as though I have lost myself. Part of me is looking at the other part, which is paralyzed.
Therapist: Actually?
Patient: No, in anticipation. During the recital I manage to keep going, but it is such agony that I never want to experience it again.

It is noteworthy that while her worst fears have never actually materialized, they have had a most seriously inhibiting and debilitating effect upon her level of function.

Therapist: And that is when you resolve never to play again?
Patient: Yes.

The next session begins with a silence that lasts over ten minutes. Then she begins.

Patient: I did not want to come today.

Therapist keeps silent since patient knows from previous experiences of this nature that the therapist is waiting for her to go on.

Patient: While I felt better during the session yesterday, after I left I became furious with you. After a long period of fulminating angrily, I realized that I just wanted to get out of performing and that you were not letting me quit.

Note that the patient has developed some capacity for reality-based self-observation. This is the result of a number of years of work, during which she would come to her session and actually rage at the therapist for forcing her into functioning situations that felt unutterably dangerous to her. By this time this element of fixed characterlogical projected assumption had been weakend by her actual experience in therapy, namely, that the therapist actually protected her autonomy. The therapist, however, continues to tread very carefully, and so asks a familiar question,

Therapist: How do I stop you?
Patient: Oh, let's not go through that charade again. I know now that you do not stop me from quitting, but it feels as though you do, and therefore, you do.
Therapist: This must give me a very strange role in your life.

The therapist here is working *with* her defenses, instead of challenging her. The therapeutic intent is to determine whether reality testing is sufficiently improved so that the patient can illuminate whether symbiotic needs still dominate and overthrow the reality that the therapist is a separate, nonthreatening person.

Patient: Yes. Sometimes I know that it was I who arranged for the recital and thereby indicated, to myself, that I do want to play and give recitals. But when it comes close, I forget all that and see you as the one forcing me to do it. This is so, even though I know better.

This is a struggle between wish, fantasy, and reality. The therapist continues to refrain from challenging the defense.

Therapist: Well, you have put up very well with my changing roles in your life.

Patient: That's because *you* are improving. I do have to say that you are getting better in the treatment!

(Laughter in which both join.)

Patient: You know that the recital takes place at the time of my session, so I will not be here next Tuesday.

Therapist: Let me see whether I can change the time on that day.

Patient: I don't want you to.

Therapist: Oh?

Patient: I don't want to risk talking to you about it. It only makes me uneasy. I was even thinking that I would like to skip the rest of my sessions between now and then so that I do not have to talk to you about it.

The patient has given evidence of an incipient process of depersonalization. The therapist bears in mind the original difficulty that had brought this woman to treatment many years ago. At that time, with enormous guilt, she recounted how terrified she had become of her own anger, which had erupted in a situation in which she found herself screaming at her nine-year-old son, "Go away, I wish you were dead." Her own frequent suicidal thoughts were much less disturbing to her, but there existed enough restitutive capacity for her to recognize the threat of disintegration of structure, in the form of being overtaken by hostility, in this precipitating event. That an only sibling had committed suicide, and that she maintained a close association with an overtly psychotic "friend," suggests serious difficulties in her own capacity for object relations. Indeed this had been the content of a long therapeutic process.

The therapist had become aware almost simultaneously of several conflicting thoughts in his own mind. First was the conviction that it would be in the patient's best interests for her to keep the appointments scheduled, because to behave as though she could not do so would be to accept that escape is more desirable, and that continued contact with the therapist is dangerous and damaging. Second, the therapist became aware of his own wish that the patient surmount the anxiety involved, that is, that she should have the necessary anxiety tolerance to enable her to work out the problem in spite of her feeling that a clear and pressing danger existed. This was followed by a third issue, the question of who should decide what the patient is capable of working on at a given moment, of how much therapeutic work can be demanded of a patient, especially when the patient feels the danger of disintegration. While she might respond by keeping her appointments, would this represent growth or compliance and the surrender of autonomy?

The concept that the lion's share of the therapeutic work lies with the patient decided the issue. The therapist chose to illuminate the dilemma but to leave the choice to the patient. This was done first by recognizing how fearful, upset, and anxious the patient was, followed by the comment that at this moment of crisis she could experience the therapist only as a threat to her equilibrium, and not as a stablizing influence. Here the therapist is attempting to help the patient shift from a projection derived from primary object experience, to achieve the capacity to recognize that her affect—fear—can be recognized now as a true displaced transference.

The therapist knew, but chose not to inform the patient, that this moment contained another opportunity to expand and effect a crucial reorganization of structure. In the past exploration of her relationship with her mother, a conviction had been impressed upon her that her mother had merely tolerated her, much preferring the older sibling, and had only "suffered" the patient's presence. This created enormous anxiety in all the patient's developing years, during which any absence of the mother led to panic. Because of her father's own problems, and also the fact that the parents had separated for a period of time, the patient had not been able to use the father as a stimulus to separation-individuation.

The current situation, therefore, replicated an opportunity for precocious and fragile independence and individuation, but once again based upon a hostile representation of the object. By canceling appointments and avoiding contact, she would feel better, and even safer, because she would not be in a situation that would confirm her fears. On the other hand, while the therapist recognized that the patient could probably be persuaded to keep her appointments, this ran the greater risk of enforcing compliance caused by anxiety rather than growth, and exactly as it had taken place with her mother. Since compliance had played much too great a part in her life, it was felt that interpretation would only have risked intellectualized compliance. The therapist chose to let matters take their own course without risking the patient's involving her intellectualized responses and defenses. This included the possibility of rebellion as well, so the therapist said nothing more.

The patient responded with the recognition that she was indeed dealing with the therapist as though he were a destabilizing force. This prompted her to decide to keep her appointments, except for the one on the actual date of the recital, the one that would have had to be changed.

Thus, she arrived at another compromise solution, albeit an improvement over past compromises. The appointment that remained canceled affirmed her past and the structure that had evolved from it, namely, that objects constitute a threat to her autonomy because they are cathected with hostility and thus cause anxiety. Simultaneously, however, since separation-individuation processes had been so burdened and incomplete, she tended toward easily surrendering her autonomy by means of compliance. The earlier appointments that she decided to keep reflected a reorganization of structure in that a new internal perception of an affirming object was coming into being, with the consequent development of a better capacity to retain autonomy even in the presence of the other person, no longer automatically negatively cathected. This is indeed progress and growth, but, typically, not in clear-cut fashion.

It remains to be added that whatever disappointment is felt that the patient remained with her reservations and had to find a compromise needs to be understood as countertransference. On the one hand, the therapist is entitled to therapeutic zeal, and it is doubtful that anyone could practice in this profession without wanting to be of help. Such appropriate wishes, however, must not be imposed upon the patient, since that would inhibit growth by enforcing compliance. This goes to the very essence of separation-individuation theory. As individuated therapists we are entitled to our feelings; those we have to keep to ourselves, apart from the patient for whom we have the professional goals of growth and individuation.

This example illustrates my perception of maximum progress. Definitive movement has taken place, although in compromise form. There is no sudden change, no "I see it all now." I have called this the "aha" fallacy. Change is taking place, but where change in psychic structure is the goal, it is more like a process of erosion.

This presentation has been an attempt to provide an overview of the ways in which internalizing processes and structural development create the various forms of transference manifestations. These reflect the state of object relations, and are found in a spectrum ranging from those transference manifestations that may be affectively revealed by interpretive efforts, that is, by semantic communication, to those that require a much longer therapeutic effort that involves an experience rather than semantic communication. At the far end of the spectrum are the primary object experiences that remain as fixed assumptions, some of which form an ineradicable core of the personality. The location in the spectrum in which the patient is found provides an important aspect of the diagnosis

REFERENCES

Blanck, R., and G. Blanck. 1977. The transference object and the real object. *Int. J. Psycho-Anal.* 58:33–44.

Blanck, G. and R. Blanck. 1979. *Ego psychology II: Psychoanalytic developmental psychology.* New York: Columbia University Press.

Eissler, K. R. 1953. The effect of the structure of the ego on psychoanalytic technique. *J. Am. Psychoanal. Assoc.* 1:104–143.

Fraiberg, S. 1963. Psychoanalysis and the education of casework. In *Ego-oriented casework: Problems and perspectives,* Howard J. Parad and Roger P. Miller (Eds.). New York: Family Service Association of America.

Freud, S. 1953–1966. *The standard edition of the complete psychological works of Sigmund Freud* (24 vols.), James Strachey (Ed.). London: Hogarth Press.

———. 1895. Studies on hysteria. *Standard edition*, vol. II. London: Hogarth Press, 1963.

———. 1917b. Mourning and melancholia. *Standard edition*, vol. XIV. London: Hogarth Press, 1957, pp. 237–258.

———. 1921. Group psychology and the analysis of the ego. *Standard edition*, vol. XVIII. London: Hogarth Press, pp. 67–143.

———. 1940. An outline of psycho-analysis. *Standard edition*, vol. XXIII. London. Hogarth Press, pp. 141–208.

Greenson, R. R. 1965b. The working alliance and the transference neurosis. *Psychoanal. Q.* 34:155–181.

Jackobson, E. 1964. *The self and the object world.* New York: International Universities Press.

Lichtenberg, J. D. 1975. The development of the sense of self. *J. Am. Psychoanal. Assoc.* 23:453–484.

Mullahy, P. 1970. *Psychoanalysis and interpersonal psychology: The contributions of Harry Stack Sullivan.* New York: Science House.

Sandler, J. 1960. The background of safety. *Int. J. Psycho-Anal.* 41:352–356.

Spitz, R. A. 1965. *The first year of life.* New York: International Universities Press.

Zetzel, E. R. 1956. Current concepts of transference. *Int. J. Psycho-Anal.* 37:369–375.

DISCUSSION

J. R. Montgomery

Reuben Blanck's work brings to mind what Freud stated in *Remembering, Repeating, and Working Through*, that handling of the transference is the principal means by which we can tame and master the compulsion to repeat and transform it into a motive for remembering. Ella Sharpe warned that failure in handling transference is really the only critical mistake in analytic work. Other mistakes can be remedied, but errors of transference are vital and not easy to alter. To recognize and handle the transference are contingent upon knowing the nature of the transference. When Douglas Orr in 1954 gave his comprehensive historical review of transference and countertransference, he stated: "It appears that further clarification of the concept of transference and issues of psychoanalytic technique must await a better integration of ego psychology and particularly more definitive knowledge of early ego development." In that same year, Phyllis Greenacre stated that the basic or primary transference originated in the mother–infant quasi-union in the first months of life. Margaret Mahler, Rene Spitz, and other psychoanalysts have confirmed Greenacre's idea of primary transference by their direct observation of the early diadic and triadic bonds and met the challenge of Orr's wish for further knowledge of early ego development. However, the observation and knowledge obtained by psychoanalytic developmentalists have needed to be applied to work with adult patients.

Blanck has extracted and creatively applied and extended the work of these psychoanalytic developmentalists to the understanding of the kind of transference and treatment approach needed in working with adult patients. He brings clarity, specificity, and precision to the term "transference" by showing that the intaking processes occurring in the primary diadic and triadic relationship lead to later transference manifestations. The kind of transference we see with our adult patients is determined by the degree to which the global intaking is successfully negotiated through the separation-individuation subphases. If the toddler has good enough endowment and smoothly separates from the primary objects, then the object representation gradually diminishes and becomes part of the self representations (selective identifications), which leads to a capacity for genuine autonomy, adaptive judgments, and relative objectivity, and thereby a capacity for true transference.

Blanck has reminded us that transference involves a certain quality of failure in reality testing; nevertheless the degree of distortion depends upon how well or inadequately the person has acquired self and object constancy. We are further told that the less-structured (borderline and narcissistic) patients do have a capacity to transfer, but the therapist is not sufficiently cathected to promote growth through interpretation. Therefore, knowing the levels of object relations of the patient indicates the type of transference and thus the therapeutic intervention indicated to promote psychological growth.

A major issue addressed is the importance of an accurate descriptive developmental diagnosis before embarking upon a course of treatment. Freud used the transference as a diagnostic tool in determining pathology in two broad categories: the transference neurosis, which indicates a capacity to displace past to present and to relive the entirety of the infantile neurosis in the transference whereby the analyst would use interpretation as the major therapeutic tool to work through the neurosis; and the narcissistic neurosis, which Freud believed was untreatable because the capacity to form a transference neurosis was lacking. Today we continue to follow Freud's view of diagnosing in the sense of using ourselves as the sensitive instrument that measures the level of object relations by trying to understand the nature of the transference. The way a patient relates and behaves with the therapist tells a great deal about the self and object representations, about the degree of differentiation and the distortions. The patient's life history is important, however, the therapist must keep in mind that the patient is remembering the events with distortions and condensations, and so the understanding of the transference is the key to diagnosing and determining treatment techniques. Blanck makes a valuable ramification of Edith Jacobson's distinction between transference, namely, the employment of displacement, and projection, a more global transference with less recognition of the other as a separate individual and less capacity for gaining or regaining perspective on oneself for self observation, reflection, and a "trail action."

Another factor in determining the diagnosis elaborated upon by Blanck is the extent to which Spitz' third organizer, namely, semantic communication, has become an "affective and effective modus operandi between self and other"—in other words the degree to which language has replaced earlier forms of communication (coenesthetic reception) in the diadic and triadic experiences. How well semantic communication develops is determined by the quality and affective balance of the primary object experiences, and if those experiences proceed with an "evenly distributed cathexis," then a balanced self and object representation occur. Also a sense of safety must be internalized for the future patient to be able to "work through" psychological problems via interpretations. The adult patient who has not more or less solidly achieved the third organizer and a sense of safety, will depend primarily upon the affective tone of the therapist, which will be of more importance than interpretations.

This leads from diagnosis to technique, and the clinical example given by Blanck would probably have been diagnosed as narcissistic neurosis by Freud, and therefore not treatable. The clinical material demonstrates how the expansion of theory has made possible the successful treatment of a patient population that previously would have been viewed as a group the psychotherapist had little to offer.

Using the contribution of psychoanalytic developmentalists as a solid ground base, Blanck has expanded both theory and technique. He has given us material for both contemplation and application.

6 Clinical Research: Encounters with Reality

Edna Adelson

A detailed case presentation of work with a family with a one-year-old blind infant who is doing poorly illustrates the naturalistic clinical research on "attachment and early ego development" under the auspices of Selma Fraiberg's Child Development Project. A combination of scholarly inquiry and sensitive clinical practice characterizes the work designed to establish and support the emotional tie between parent and child and build in essential experience so as to minimize misunderstanding and underestimation of the infant's special needs. The research, conducted on home visits, permitted innovations in clinical intervention that helped this family and others toward a better future.

DISCUSSION by Gerda Schulman From the perspective of a family therapist, Schulman broadens the focus from the mother–child dyad to emphasize attention to the father as coparent, the needs of the sibling, and the potential neglect of the spouse system (marriage),which tends to occur in families with children who have special needs. She notes the need for preventive work with the family at transition points when reworking the issue is required.

Work with young children is intense and compelling. And work with troubled infants can feel even more so. When the sense of urgency threatens to disrupt the work, the interplay of theory and practice can provide insight and steady encouragement. Selma Fraiberg understood this. This chapter reflects on the beginnings of the clinical research she directed at the Child Development Project in the late 1960s and the 1970s.

One could gain a better sense of the climate of such work by spending some hours baby watching. You would look at a film of happy, healthy babies moving through ordinary moments of daily life—and while you watched the film, I would watch you. Most often I would see an audience comfortably tuned into the baby's world, unconsciously letting their every expressions mirror what was happening on the screen. There would be a unity, a feeling that things are generally all right despite small ups and downs.

There is another set of films we ought to watch to remind us of what we actually see in clinical work. These are films of troubled infants and toddlers. Such films are difficult to watch. Whenever we see pictures of babies suffering from prolonged deprivation or neglect, babies who do not give the usual social signs, toddlers whose development is delayed or uneven or somehow distorted, then the faces in the audience tell me another story. People look anxious. There is restlessness in the room. Sometimes there are quiet tears. As the film proceeds, faces turn away because nothing is more unbearable than watching the unhappiness of a little child and feeling helpless to do anything about it. What I see happening in the audience at those times is what I believe can also happen in a family. When parents are faced with a constant picture of an infant's distress, and when they feel helpless in their own deep despair, they too must detach in some measure and protect themselves by turning away.

Selma did not turn away. She had the courage to look closely for the smallest signs of capacity and hope. With the mind of a scholar and the heart of a clinician, she could observe disorganization and missing connections without feeling disrupted or disconnected herself. She sought evidence of attachment, of affect, or attempts at adaptation—and used them with clinical inspiration to set change in motion. She combined her training in social work and child psychoanalysis with a tireless intellectual energy to develop a series of research and training programs at the University of Michigan and the University of California. For all those who knew her and worked with her, it was a time of rare adventure.

I joined the Child Development Project in 1967. The ongoing research was titled "Attachment and Early Ego Development" and our subjects were infants who were blind from birth and their families. We had many questions and very few answers. By way of instruction I was offered several slim volumes of heavy text: Piaget, Spitz, Werner, Bowlby, and Ainsworth. These were fine guides to theories of development and attachment, but they contained nothing about the specific behavior or development of blind babies and nothing about conduct on home visits. There was another kind of instruction: the staff spent hours watching a few segments from films of the first infants in the study. We ran them in slow motion, taking hours to argue over what we had seen, using the results to frame a code to clarify and organize the observations. And we argued about their significance for practice and theory.

Then, well before I felt ready for it, I was assigned to a family with a one-year-old blind infant who was not doing well. I was given generous advice on how to behave as a visiting research clinician: look for early signs of attachment, distress, pleasure; indications of a sense of self and other; the emergence of object concept in the Piagetian sense and of object permanence in the psychoanalytic sense. Watch for the use of large and small musculature, listen for early vocalizations. Be sure to meet the different expectations of the family, staff, and research sponsor. Be relaxed and spontaneous and get complete naturalistic observations for an hour on each weekly home visit. Back at the office, dictate ten pages of narrative data that preserve sequence, context, and detail in a form that keeps observation, report, and inference clearly differentiated.

Eventually all the staff learned this disciplined baby watching and it was good preparation for the later work with other groups of infants at risk for abuse, neglect, and severe prematurity. The story of Karen and her family will show what it was like to shuttle between office and home for encounters with the realities of research and practice. Their problems highlight the difficulties often posed by congenital blindness. At the same time, they point to the role of vision in linking partners to one another, in building pathways to a world of objects, words, and ideas, in integrating varieties of experience.

WORKING WITH KAREN

Karen is blind. When I first saw her at 11 months, her parents described her as being "no trouble at all"—and so she was, since she slept 20 hours a day and did little but suck her pacifier when awake. She seldom laughed or cried. She did not like to be held and was unhappy anywhere except lying in her crib or sitting in her swing or her bouncing seat where no toys could be kept within reach. The back of her head was bald. Her hands looked peculiar, useless. Most of the time they were up near her shoulders, bent back at the wrists, half closed. Occasionally when she was upright, she would sweep the space behind her head in a strange, apparently purposeless way. She presented a frightening example of failure to progress, the result of months of unintentional maternal and sensory deprivation. Her parents were as deprived as she was.

Mr. and Mrs. Cook are a stable, working-class couple who were then in their early 20s. Karen, their first child, was three months premature; she weighed only two pounds, three ounces, at birth, and it was two months before she could leave the hospital. Her worried parents tried to hold her, but she was stiff. She seemed to reject their attention and she did not look at their faces. She was not the way they expected a baby to be, and they could not understand what was wrong. Soon Mrs. Cook became pregnant again. After a while, they wondered if Karen could see, and took her to a doctor who assured them that nothing was the matter. Not until Karen was four months old was the blindness officially confirmed and diagnosed as retrolental fibroplasia. She was totally blind. Confused, afraid, depressed, and angry, the Cooks cared as best they could for their sightless first child while they awaited the birth of their second child.

When Karen was just eight and a half months old, her sister Patty was born, also premature, but not quite so small. Patty spent one month in the hospital, a tense time for the mother and father, who were faced again with all-too-familiar fears about a tiny infant and possible blindness, and who had nowhere to turn for help.

In spite of their anxiety and fear, they did what they thought was right for both children. However, serious as they were about being good parents, and as much as they wanted and loved their babies, they were quite ignorant about early infant development. They described infancy as a dull time when babies only eat and sleep, and that was what the girls did. As Karen's first birthday drew near, they waited patiently for her to walk and talk, but were beginning to doubt that she would. A pediatric ophthalmologist who examined Karen referred the family to the Child Development Project, which had recently begun at the University of Michigan.

On visits to observe Karen, I also saw Patty, and watching her, came to understand what Karen's first year may have been like. Patty's days were monotonous and understimulating. Within the walls of her bassinet or tilted back in her infant seat, she had nothing to look at, nothing to play with. Her bottle was propped. She had too much sleep, too little handling. Unable to ignore Patty's plight, I made suggestions and brought her toys. They were not used. She began to show many similarities to the institution babies described by Provence and Lipton (1962). At seven months an attractive toy was dangled before her. She looked at it eagerly, moved toward it with her eyes, her mouth, and her head, but her hands remained out at her sides; she did not even begin to reach for it.

Patty was deprived and delayed in several ways, as Karen had also been. Nevertheless her future was not in jeopardy to the same extent because she was not blind. She could see her mother and something of the world around her. She was cuddly and comprehensible to her family, and when she grew too big and active to be contained any longer, she began to reach and move toward what she saw, and came alive—a little late, but definitely on her way.

For Karen such an easy change was impossible. For a blind child the world will not suddenly reveal itself after 11 impoverished months. Instead the natural increase in motor energy is more likely to lead to repetitive dead-end behaviors, which are *not* due to the blindness, since they also occur in disturbed sighted children, but which may come about as the understimulated blind child attempts to adapt to restricted and fragmented experience.

Details of our research and educational programs are reported elsewhere (Fraiberg, 1977). We have found that the milestones of human attachment should be as they are for any child: smiling, preference for the mother, reaction to a stranger, all at the usual times. Sleeping and eating patterns and early speech patterns should also be no different. Creeping and walking are usually delayed in the blind child, but good control of the body in other ways should not be late. Since touch and hearing do not automatically compensate for the missing sense of sight, special care must be taken to ensure from the start that the hands come together at midline, that the fingers become adept and alert, and that sounds come to have meaning. An important finding of our research is that reach on sound, which is as important to the blind child as reach on sight is to the sighted child, may not occur until the age of ten or 11 months, which is five to six months later than reach on sight. And until it does occur, there will be no attempt to seek something out of reach, no creeping, no mobility.

Our central concerns are to establish and support the emotional tie between parent and child, and to build in essential learning experiences of hand and ear during the prolonged period of immobility when the blind infant cannot seek them, when special needs may be misunderstood or underestimated.

We had been able to do this for blind infants whom we saw very early in the first year. Would it be possible to help Karen? There were so many ways in which she resembled older autistic blind children. Her appearance at 11 months and what her parents told us about her infancy sounded too much like other descriptions and histories in the literature on the disturbed blind. Although no developmental scales have been standardized for infants totally blind from birth, we knew from our own research sample, and from the study by Norris and colleagues (1957), that Karen was functioning at a seriously retarded level. Her intellectual and emotional development was imperiled by a gross lack of appropriate sensory stimulation and, even more seriously, by the lack of a close and affectionate relationship with her mother. However, there were several indications that change was still possible. First, her mother and father wanted help. Then there was no evidence from recent medical examinations to indicate other handicaps or brain damage. More important was what we saw in Karen herself. Karen had reacted strongly to her mother's absence at the time of Patty's birth; she had slept even more, eaten less, and her vocalizations had almost stopped. To us this meant she was seeking an attachment. She did smile when spoken to. Her muscle tone was good as she sat in her bouncing seat. Even her awkard hands offered hopeful cues: they came together to hold her bottle. And when I left my hand beside hers, I could feel her fingers move ever so slightly on mine in tentative exploration. She did not reject the outside world—but she had not yet discovered it.

INVOLVING THE MOTHER

Work with Mrs. Cook involved sympathetic support, education, and some demonstration. Therapy was not involved, but a clinical understanding of her needs and feelings was always important. Many times it was simpler to do things instead of talking about them since she was not comfortable in conversation.

Using the details of informal ordinary events, we searched for some way to bring mother and baby together, to help them begin to share small spontaneous moments with pleasure. The home visits, which lasted an hour, were once a week for a while, and then twice monthly. The sessions were filmed monthly.* The notes of the visits and the films were regularly reviewed by the project staff.

We noted that Karen would let me hold her for play, but that she was seldom held by her mother. We thought the regular bottle feedings might be a route to bring about change. If Mrs. Cook could hold Karen, they would have many times together each day. Mrs. Cook listened politely while I described what it meant to a child to be held close, listening to her mother's voice as she enjoyed her bottle, to touch and to be touched, to hear and to be heard. But she continued her routine of propping Karen's bottle beside her and leaving her alone to drink it. When I pressed Mrs. Cook to feed Karen on her lap while I was there, she did so, but mother and child were clumsy, stiff with apprehension. Mrs. Cook looked stony and cold; Karen looked blank, empty. This was not going to work at all, so we had to rethink the strategy. Reality was still the true test of theory and of clinical skill.

Somehow I had to find a bridge between mother and child without usurping Mrs. Cook's central role. On each visit I spent

---

*A case history of Karen from 12 to 20 months is available on 16mm film from the University of Michigan Media Center.

a few minutes sitting on the floor to play with Karen on my lap. I introduced her to the toys I had brought, while making my own unobtrusive assessments. Karen enjoyed these play sessions. Maybe this would be a way Mrs. Cook could more easily hold and enjoy her child, but she was making no moves in this direction. She remained depressed and doubtful. One morning, as Karen played with a bell on my lap, she made some small sound, which I firmly said meant that she wanted her mother. Somehow I stood up with Karen and the bell and the toy box and deposited them all on Mrs. Cook's lap. Through it all Karen continued her fascinated exploration of the bell. Mrs. Cook, in her intuitive effort to balance everything, enclosed Karen in her arms and soon was drawn into the play herself. She pulled on the bell gently and held Karen fast; their heads touched and they both smiled. They were comfortable with each other and together they went on to explore the rest of the toys. It was a start. Playing with toys, with possibilities of active exchange, and demonstrations of intelligence connected them.

Mrs. Cook was shy and found conversation a strain. She seldom spoke to Karen to tell her what was happening. It was difficult to convince her that Karen paid attention to her mother's words, that Karen could use language to make sense of an invisible world. The natural course of events provided a clear demonstration. The family dog was scolded all day long. The sudden sharp commands made me flinch every time. One day, just as Karen learned to sit by herself on the floor, the dog wandered by and Mrs. Cook shouted angrily, "Get out of here!" Karen froze, trembled, and began to cry. I comforted her and she resumed playing. Later a fierce warning was again shouted at the dog, but this time the dog's name had preceded the shout. Karen quieted for a moment, but she did not seem afraid and she did not cry.

There was small hope of getting Mrs. Cook to stop scolding the dog. Perhaps this regular event could prove useful. I commented on the two episodes and asked Mrs. Cook to let me know how Karen reacted at other times. Did she notice a difference when the dog's name was used? Intrigued by Karen's potential cleverness, Mrs. Cook tested this hypothesis completely before the next visit. She watched her daughter attentively. She reported with great satisfaction that Karen had never cried when the dog was scolded by name. Her parents were impressed and life became a little more predictable for Karen. Karen also became more predictable to her parents. Mrs. Cook said Karen thought about a lot of things and understood more than you might guess. They were more in touch with one another.

After four weekly visits, several changes indicated to us that Karen's daily routine was improving and that her parents were more assured of her adequacy. When Mrs. Cook recognized Karen's boredom, she no longer treated it as fatigue and did not hurry her to bed. As a result Karen's sleep decreased dramatically. She took only two naps and her bald spot faded. Her hands had not yet relaxed but she rolled about and could get onto her hands and knees. She sat comfortably on her mother's lap, and could also sit unsupported on the floor. This was considerable progress, but her parents could not understand why she did not try to crawl or walk right away.

Like most people, Karen's parents could not recognize the unique conceptual problems faced by a blind child. It takes more effort and time to organize inner and outer experience without vision to aid memory and to confirm and reconfirm what is perceived. For example, how did Karen make sense of the space around her and her place in that space? An interesting clue lay in the odd sweeping gesture Karen made behind her head when she was standing up. For several weeks it remained a puzzle. Then, one day, after Karen had lost her uneasiness about playing on the floor, she was lying on her back shaking a rattling cube, when it fell from one hand and landed beside her ear. She moved her arm repeatedly back and forth between her shoulder and head, trying to grasp the cube she could feel with her fingertips. We understood that Karen, with many months of experience on her back was conducting a perfectly good search based on past successes with fallen bottles and pacifiers.

I did not appreciate what all this meant until later during the same visit. After Karen had played with a musical rattle while supine on the floor, I took it from her and sounded it beside her. Lured by the musical note, she rolled over onto her stomach. I shook the rattle in front of her. Karen accurately located the rattle by the sound, stretched her arm straight toward it, and touched it with her fingertips, but could not quite grasp it. This reaction confirmed that her physiological maturation had advanced, and that refined hearing was now available to her to be used for reality testing, communications, and self/object differentiation. Her subsequent curious behavior, however, revealed her mental dilemma. Instead of reaching again to the spot where she had just felt the rattle, Karen bent her arm and brought it back to sweep the space between shoulder and head. It was another attempt at a search, and it was quite useless under the circumstances. Yet she repeated the movements, even after the rattle was sounded again and she had reached forward once more to touch it. Her behavior appeared senseless, irrational to us, yet it made sense to Karen. In Karen's limited world, there was only one place to find things. She knew that in her bed fallen things always landed on the mattress toward her back. Although the floor was now beneath her stomach, she continued to direct her search toward her back. She could unite sound and touch and infer the rattle's existence outside herself, yet she could not appreciate the new relationship involving her body, the floor, and the toy. Words alone could not help her with this puzzle.

Karen needed time to learn the new possibilities of her own body. She needed to learn that, if she reached out through the darkness and the silence, there was much to be found at her fingertips. She needed to enjoy play that would give her reliable and accurate mental images of the outer world. This much we understood from theory. Experience and hunch led us to a solution. We lent the family a playpen and for the next month Karen used this enclosed space to discover what she needed to know about herself and about inanimate objects. With the playpen I left some toys: one from a toy store, one I had made, one an ordinary kitchen item. By the next visit Mrs. Cook had bought a better toy, invented a more interesting gadget, and found many kitchen things that Karen liked. Mrs. Cook was also sure Karen preferred those her mother chose for her. Led on by an active interest in all these new playthings, Karen thoroughly explored the possibilities within the playpen. It now made sense to search persistently and in different ways for what she wanted and, as she searched, she moved ever more efficiently, first on her stomach, then on hands and knees. Soon she was able to pull herself up to a standing position, initiating these activities herself. While she played, she babbled.

BUILDING INDEPENDENCE

For the next half year, Karen made progress in many areas. Gross motor changes were rapid and much valued by the family. Once Karen had learned her way about the playpen, she was ready for larger territory. At 13 months she crept across the living room. One month later she knew the entire house. Her mother said, "I never know where she is now." Soon she was climbing onto everything. At 17 months she took her first steps, and by 18 months she preferred walking to creeping. She was upright and active.

As soon as Karen became active and mobile, the sweeping gesture near her head disappeared. Gradually she brought her hands down from shoulder level, and they became more open. When there was momentary confusion around her, when a stranger approached, or when her mother scolded her sharply, her hands went back briefly to the old posture, a signal to us that she was uncertain or afraid. If Karen's development had not been altered, it is likely these behaviors would have persisted in their inutile forms. Seen several years in the future, they would have been difficult to understand, and even more difficult to change. They would have been tagged as undesirable habits or blindisms.

In this same half year, other very important advances were occurring that alternately pleased and confused the Cooks or that revealed continuing conflict. Earlier the Cooks had felt rebuffed and hurt by Karen's stiffness and unresponsiveness. Now Karen could make her feelings quite clear: she could not do without her mother, whom she would follow or seek over any distance, around any obstacle throughout the house.

Karen's move toward her mother was wholehearted and unmistakable. Her mother's reaction to this was cautious. Mrs. Cook did not enjoy physical closeness. She did not find it easy to show affection, at least not with visitors present. Her voice was more often stern than soft. She was more comfortable with older than with very young children. At first it was hard for her to understand and accept Karen's need for her. Karen had disappointed and rejected her. Karen would have to make most of the advances. Again we had to respect the family's deepest feelings and private reservations.

Sometimes I spoke for Karen, expressing what I thought she felt when she looked happy or seemed sad, always calling attention to her reactions to her mother. Over and over I pointed out how Karen smiled at her mother's voice and quieted at mine. I also spoke to Karen, telling her how delighted I was when something I did pleased her, and how discouraging it was when I did not know the right thing to do. After a while, when Karen teethed or had a cold, her mother could take her on her lap to comfort her silently and Karen snuggled and enjoyed the closeness.

At 14 months Karen tried to stay near her mother, creeping after her, playing beside her, clinging to her. She began to show separation anxiety and could not be left with relatives or friends when her mother shopped. The Cooks felt Karen was becoming spoiled and needed stricter treatment and more separations. Drawing upon theory, we explained that Karen was making up for what she had missed; once she was assured of human ties and could hold her mother more permanently in her mind, she could move away at her own pace. With this explanation and reassurance, Mr. and Mrs. Cook were able to give Karen the close contact she needed and help her work her way through this period. By 16 months she was more tolerant of strangers and had less need to know constantly where her mother was. At 17 months Karen took off on her own, eager to explore any and all new situations. She was independent and confident. She was walking. To her parents this meant she was alright. A month later, for the first time, we heard Mrs. Cook identify herself as "Mama" to her child.

It was in the delayed use of the word "Mama," and the reluctant acceptance of Karen's attempts at speech, that Mrs. Cook's continuing hurt, doubt, and anger showed itself. Karen's language was the last accomplishment to meet with her mother's recognition and approval. From what Mrs. Cook reported, Karen's vocalizations had deteriorated in the months before I first saw her. When I first met her, she no longer laughed or cried, and only a few whispers were left of the earlier babbling.

After the visits began, as Karen became more responsive and comprehensible, her mother began to speak to her. She still spoke loudly to Karen, almost as if she thought a blind child could not hear well. But the loud voice seemed mainly to express a continual anger. It was interesting to note that when Karen resumed babbling at 13 months, it was with the same intensity and force one heard in her mother's voice. At 14 months Karen would obey "no, no." At 15 months she "talked" all the time in sentences of jargon, with little meaning, but with fine conversational inflection. She acquired two new words, "Dada" and "Sissy," but no word yet for mother. Her father spoke to her gently and always found some meaning in what she said. He thought she was talking quite well. Her mother thought she was hardly talking at all.

I could hear Karen's new words and questions clearly. However, most of her attempts were ignored by her mother. Mrs. Cook's response always was, "What did you say? I can't understand you." Suggestions were made of other ways to respond to Karen, but at that point Mrs. Cook could not support her child's language development. It was not until Karen was two that she began to use the word "Mama" freely herself. Then, gradually, Mrs. Cook could hear and understand the other things Karen said. Finally, when Karen was two and a half, her mother began to talk comfortably to her, picking up her phrases or questions and giving answers that led Karen into more speech. From then on Karen's speech improved rapidly. She never merely echoed what was said to her. She quickly mastered the use of "I" and "you." As a matter of fact, her use of language became quite impressive.

IN SUMMARY

To sum up, at 18 months things were going well and by 24 months we were even more assured of Karen's adequacy. Karen was feeding herself and sleeping a normal amount. We no longer feared for her future. Our initial concern had been that without a change she might have remained body-centered, unresponsive to others, unaware of the external world, eventually becoming uneducable or autistic. Now, with strong affectional ties clearly demonstrated, with concept of permanent object well established for people and for things, with gross and fine motor behaviors and language all progressing, and with no nonadaptive stereotyped behaviors, Karen's development placed her well above average in a sample of congenitally blind children.

Without theories to guide us, we could not have made sense of Karen's behaviors. In searching for answers to questions about stages of development, the unfolding of comprehension and emotion, the inner organization of experience, and adaptation to the external world, we found we could help this family and many others find a chance for a better future. A similar combination of scholarly inquiry and sensitive clinical practice guided the work reported in *Clinical Studies in Infant Mental Health* (Fraiberg, 1980).

Selma Fraiberg was convinced that naturalistic clinical research could be conducted on home visits in a way that permitted innovations in clinical intervention for an unserved population of infants and their families. Her contributions to the field of infant psychiatry are a testimony to her success. We are all in her debt as we continue to set directions for study, training, service, and new social policy.

REFERENCES

Ainsworth, M. D. S. 1967. *Infancy in Uganda.* Baltimore: Johns Hopkins Press.

Bowlby, J. 1952. *Deprivation of maternal care.* Geneva: World Health Organization.

Fraiberg, S. 1977. *Insights from the blind.* New York: Basic Books.

———. 1980. *Clinical studies in infant mental health* (in collaboration with Louis Fraiberg). New York: Basic Books.

Norris, M., F. Brodie, and P. T. Spaulding. 1957. *Blindness in children.* Chicago: University of Chicago Press.

Piaget, J. 1954. *The construction of reality in the child.* New York: Basic Books.

———. 1952. *Origins of intelligence in children.* New York: International Universities Press.

Provence, S., and R. C. Lipton. 1962. *Infants in institutions.* New York: International Universities Press.

Spitz, R. A. 1965. *The first year of life: A psychoanalytic study of normal and deviant development of object relations* (in collaboration with W. G. Cobliner). New York: International Universities Press.

——. 1957. *No and yes.* New York: International Universities Press.

Werner, H. 1948. *Comparative psychology of mental development.* New York: International Universities Press.

DISCUSSION

Gerda Schulman

In her touching, human, and very lucid account, Adelson has more descriptively than quantitatively demonstrated concepts reflective of Selma Fraiberg's work and writings. As author-therapist, Adelson has permitted us to share in the process of initiating changes through her painstaking observation of the mother–child dyad, observations which in turn guided her actions through a consistent, confirming, validating, and discarding of assumptions. In this sense the treatment process is *ad hoc* research as it demonstrates or validates the intricate process of achieving change.

"Encounters with Reality" accurately reflects a treatment process that is grounded in reality, the reality that shapes a relationship between a mother and a handicapped child (blind from birth) and that is profoundly influenced, touched, and guided by a therapist, who in turn is guided by their attitude and responses, including those that reflect "resistance." From a system's point of view, any behavior on the part of a family member that blocks change serves to alert the therapist that change came too rapidly or in ways the family cannot yet absorb. Thus Adelson recognized that at a certain point, Karen needed to win her mother over, and so she encouraged the child, instead of pushing the mother to go beyond her ability.

There is a refreshing absence of the critical or arrogant "know better than thou" attitude that some experts display, even in the light of a stark family tragedy with its inherent and reactive limitations. Throughout the therapist, who, like the mother, struggles for answers, shows deep respect for the parent's role and plight. She never blames the mother or is critical of her failure and later slowness in responding to the child's movement. Neither does she ever fall into the trap of doing for the mother what the mother can do herself. She serves as the mother's enabler and not her substitute. Never intrusive, she is ever alert to the slightest sign of readiness on the part of the mother to respond to and do for her child. In a poignant episode that dramatizes a breakthrough in the relationship, the therapist deposits Karen who has "discovered" a toy into the lap of the mother, facilitating a moment of rare intimacy between the mother and child.

Education is rightly part of treatment. It takes place through modeling in a subtle way, making suggestions, and sparingly giving explanations regarding the difference between the development of a handicapped and a normal child. Like the parent, the reader-clinician can learn much from Adelson's discussion of how a visually handicapped child learns differently about space and how to maneuver the environment successfully.

One of the most widely used concepts in family therapy is the notion of behavior as purposeful. Similarly, Adelson avoids labeling seemingly inappropriate behavior as a sign of retarded development. She never gives up until she deciphers the mystery of Karen's world. Once this is done, she finds ways to guide Karen into more useful behavior, which eventually is conveyed to the mother, who then is able to build on what the therapist had begun.

While Karen remains the focus and target of therapy, Adelson, following in Selma Fraiberg's footsteps, recognizes that children, especially young and handicapped ones, can be helped only if transactions in relation to them shift. Thus the focus of intervention is the mother–child dyad, a basic subgroup of the family.

Adelson noted the debt we owe to Selma Fraiberg as we continue to set directions for study, training, service, and new social policy. In the spirit of this tribute and challenge, I would like to propose, as a family therapist, the consideration of some additional avenues; if pursued, these could prove most advantageous not only for Karen, but for her family as well. While it is true that the mother is crucial to the child, the father remains a shadowy figure, too little involved throughout; this is also true for a sister whose life will forever be influenced by the fact that Karen is blind, and, although younger, may be thrust into a position of being her sister's caretaker. She, as well as the rest of the family, will have to learn to find a way to live with "a grief that never goes away." In general the parents are treated as if they were undifferentiated, and only much later it turns out that the father is more pleased with and cognizant of Karen's progress than the mother. I suspect that this may be related to the undue burden on the mother, who not only needed to learn how to deal with a child like Karen, but who had two babies in quick succession. A slight allusion is made to some negative reaction on the part of both parents when, to the delight of the therapist, the child Karen becomes more of a person, and hence more demanding and more draining of mother's resources, as she changes from being passively docile into a lively but naturally more difficult child. Would this not be the time when the father would need to cocarry some of the parental responsibility for the child (children) while at the same time more attention should be paid to the neglect of the marriage, a neglect that tends to occur more often in families with children who have special needs? This mother is expected to be satisfied with what she gets when Karen becomes increasingly responsive. Will this be enough for her? Looking into the future, and in spite of the impressive catching up on the part of Karen, who has become a "normal" blind child, one wonders as to the continued effect of the handicap of one member on the family as a whole, notably the well sibling, who so easily could become the parental child.

The therapist demonstrates so well the importance of early and appropriate intervention in relation to a "child in need and at high risk," but the family, too, would benefit equally from some preventive work. This would allow them to grow and develop through the normal and special vicissitudes of life, in which at every transition point the issue will need to be dealt with anew.

Selma Fraiberg, through her work and writings, challenged us to learn while we help. Adelson's work impressively testifies to her integration of that philosophy. In outlining some additional paths for intervention by working from the case Adelson described, I have tried to add another dimension to this heritage.

7 American Casework in Europe: Historical Highlights

Katherine A. Kendall

The marriage of dynamic psychology and democracy as represented in American casework and its contribution to the transformation of European social work after World War II is the focus here. Kendall draws upon her international experience in social work education and the literature to document this process of change.

Renowned British social work educator Dame Eileen Young-husband once said to me: "Social work came to age when the Americans got Sigmund Freud all mixed up with the Declaration of Independence." The more I thought about this, the more I realized that this gem was not just another of the clever remarks for which Dame Eileen was famous. The Post-World War II transformation of European social work was systematically influenced by the marriage of dynamic psychology and democracy. In the United States, the product of this alliance was casework. The process by which American casework impacted social work education and practice is the theme of this chapter.

IMPACT OF WORLD WAR II

World War II left in its wake a heavy burden, not only of physical destruction, but of personal havoc such as broken homes, loss of parents, loss of children, physical and emotional wounds, disruption of families through separation, and divided loyalties. The litany of hurt and deprivation could go on and on, but a checklist is not needed to establish that despite the stories of heroic deeds, and there were many, war can never be anything but dehumanizing. The malignant impact of Nazism added to the malaise. That is the setting in which European social work functioned in the late 1940's.

Before the advent of American casework. European and American social work had certain common characteristics, but also many differences. In most countries social work rested upon and proceeded from social legislation designed to eliminate or alleviate poverty. In that respect Europe was considerably in advance of the United States, and perhaps achieved a greater measure of general social good. It followed from this primary concern with economic and social provisions that social work practice consisted in the main of program implementation, use of legislation, interpretation of regulations, manipulation of the environment, and control of social factors. Preparation for this practice was based on a general cultural education and drew heavily on the social sciences. There was not much in the way of methodology beyond helpful hints in the classroom, use of procedures in agencies, and whatever else students were able to pick up in an apprenticeship type of field work.

CASEWORK COMES TO EUROPE

The stage is now set for the grand entrance of American casework upon the European scene. Note, however, that the idea of casework, and the word itself (two words then), were both in common use in Europe. In fact one of the early but short-lived training programs—the School of Sociology established in 1903 by the London Charity Organization Society—described casework as an essential element of field work in the following terms: "Case work. Study of case papers, home visiting, inquiry work, interviewing, preparing a plan for assistance and devising means for carrying out the plan, reporting on applications and advising as to suitable treatment." (United Nations 1958, p. 111). Mary Richmond's *Social Diagnosis* (1917) was well known in Britain, and to a lesser extent in other countries. In preparing this chapter, I came across a description of the impact of American relief activities in southern and eastern Europe after World War I. The way in which U.S. social workers handled disaster situations, organized communities for reconstructive effort, and helped to rebuild shattered lives was contrasted with what was described as haphazard alms giving, spying, repression, and helpless indifference to suffering. A desire to learn more about this American approach led to the organization in 1919 of a summer course for social workers in Prague and the text was *Social Diagnosis* (Hurlbutt, 1920).

It is tempting to infer from the historical highlights just mentioned that American social work practice finds its most enthusiastic acceptance in other lands after catastrophic wars, death, and destruction. Certainly it was through the work of American social workers in United Nations Relief and Rehabilitation Administration and then through the social welfare services and other activities of the United Nations in Europe following World War II that many European social workers became aware of a missing element in their approach to people and their problems. Dr. Jan de Jongh of the Netherlands, another internationally renowned social work educator, voiced the challenge in a major address at the first postwar International Congress of Schools of Social Work held in Paris in 1950. He said: "It seems to me that for all the European schools now the time has come for a confrontation of their educational content with American casework and its implications." (p. 21).

He went on to analyze the differences between American casework and European social work practice, stressing the following potential contributions of the American approach (de Jongh, 1951, pp. 24–27):

—Replacing the intuitive, common sense, good heart approach much in evidence in Europe with a scientifically based methodology.

—Creating awareness that social difficulties frequently have emotional components and that effective social treatment requires a recognition and understanding of human feelings and attitudes that lie beneath superficial attitudes.

—Developing the ability to diagnose, making use of interviewing techniques that give clients sufficient comfort and confidence to disclose the real character of their problems.

—Replacing the condescending autocratic and condescending materialistic attitude with an essentially democratic, nonjudgmental attitude, and acting always in cooperation with the client.

—Emphasizing the conscious and responsible use of a professional relationship, as something different from a friendly and sympathetic approach.

THE AGONY OF CHANGE

The initial response to this challenge to European schools to confront their teaching in the light of American casework was, as one would expect, not universally enthusiastic. The ambivalence was well described by Dame Eileen Younghusband and Professor Majorie Smith of Canada in a paper presented in 1953 at the First Annual Program Meeting of the Council on Social Work Education.

> Casework is regarded in Europe as being essentially an American product. It is viewed by Europeans with both fascination and misgiving. Fascination because they feel there is something here only imperfectly understood which may have great value, or, on the contrary, be full of danger. Moreover, they are unsure whether it is a home-grown product for home consumption only, or whether it is capable of export, with or without modification, to other parts of the world. They have an uneasy feeling that this is an important new development whose implications they should consider, but their misgivings start with the general reluctance of the Europeans to have their culture, as they would see it, Americanized. . . . (p. 86)

The cultural factor loomed large, as it always does. Other writers noted, for example, the value placed by Americans on things that are new, whether they are automobiles or theories, assuming that if something is new, it is better. In Europe, on the other hand, it was just the opposite. To replace what existed, anything new had to prove its value. The fact that so much of American casework literature was based on psychoanalytic theory also created problems. Psychoanalysis was not accepted in Europe as it was in the United States. In fact this was a bitter bone of contention. I was personally made aware of this when I was told, in connection with a paper I was preparing for a European casework seminar, to avoid all reference to psychoanalysis and to use instead the term "dynamic psychology."

Despite the reserve and the resentment expressed by some, the acceptance of American casework by leading social workers throughout Europe became the wave of the future. Dr. de Jongh (1953, p. 17) described the overriding value of American casework as fostering:

—A truly democratic attitude toward people.
—A truly scientific approach.
—A truly dynamic readiness to look at one's self and one's role in the helping process.

Social workers traveling in both directions across the Atlantic contributed to the spread of casework teaching by Americans in Eupope and absorption by Europeans in the study of casework in the United States. A series of casework seminars organized in all the major countries of Europe by the European Regional Office of the United Nations proved to be the most effective means of dispelling doubts and disseminating knowledge about casework philosophy, principles, and techniques. These seminars were among the most imaginative ever undertaken by the United Nations, and the credit for them goes to Marguerite Pohek, an American psychiatric social worker, who conceived and ran the program.

The way in which the seminars were organized not only involved social work educators and practitioners in a learning situation, but also created what would now be described as a media event. They received wide press and radio attention. Government officials were involved in the arrangements. Agency personnel and interested lay people were given an opportunity to find out what this new methodology in social welfare was all about. Support for the movement was sought at the highest levels. For example, Queen Juliana met, entertained, and talked with the group when the seminars were held in Holland. All of this contributed to the transformation of European social work and social work education.

PRACTICE AND CURRICULUM STRESS

In the United States, the agencies spearheaded the development of dynamically oriented casework. In Europe the schools of social work took the lead, and when one remembers the difficulties involved in revising a curriculum, it is amazing how quickly they progressed. Consider what needed to be done. Eileen Younghusband put it this way at a United Nations seminar in 1952: In one sense "casework *is* the curriculum." She later added: "If we look more closely at the dangerous earlier statement that casework is the curriculum, we may get a better understanding of how it should and could be taught, though we must pause to notice that, curiously enough, the statement that casework is the curriculum is quite different from saying that the curriculum is casework" (p. 162).

This is an important distinction. What she was saying in effect is that the introduction of American casework affected every course in the curriculum. Casework instruction would not rest easily, for example, on a psychological base consisting in the main of experimentation with rats. Adding a casework course unrelated to other courses was, in her view, the way *not* to teach this new subject. She urged the organization of a professional course of two years' duration that would include relatively few subjects but all would rest on a good working knowledge of people and society and be closely related to supervised practice. How to provide the envisaged practice when very few European agencies could offer educational supervision was a major problem in all countries. It was immediately recognized that while students needed sound theoretical instruction, no amount of theory alone could make them competent as caseworkers. To assimilate what they were learning about human behavior, to use what they were taught about interviewing and other techniques, and, most important, to experience the development of the client–worker relationship and to grow in self-awareness, supervised casework practice was an essential element of this new approach.

Holland led the way in developing the means to overcome what in most European countries was the greatest obstacle to the introduction of this new type of casework into social work practice. In 1951 a one-year casework and supervision course was launched for qualified and experienced workers, who spent three days in the classroom and three days in the field under supervisors provided, to a large extent, by American or American-trained Dutch psychiatric social workers. Throughout Europe schools interested in developing casework eagerly turned to Canada and the United States for the help they needed in changing the curriculum and transforming practice in the field. In the beginning they also used American case material, and that had many drawbacks. Fortunately the United Nations responded to this need. Largely through the volunteer efforts of a group of European casework teachers, a pool of case materials was assembled in French and English to serve until each country had its own teaching material.

For North Americans this was the heyday of international cooperation and exchange in social work. Casework teachers were recruited by individual schools on various kinds of sabbatical arrangements, by individual countries under the Fulbright or other bilateral programs, and by the United Nations for short-term assignments as contributors at European casework seminars or for longer term appointments in Europe, Asia, and Latin America as consultants and advisors. Remembering the cornucopia of international opportunities available in the 1950s and 1960s, it is no wonder that American social work educators tended to develop a sense of mission about their role as teachers to the world.

The traffic was anything but one way. Opportunities for European social workers to study in schools of social work or to develop competence in casework practice and supervision through various types of training programs were available from many government and private sources, but the United Nations, through its social welfare fellowship program, led the way. The 1950s and early 1960s were thus a period of remarkable growth for social work and social work education. They were also a period of strong international solidarity fostered by the many technical assistance programs in social welfare and the genuine belief of social work leaders everywhere in the ultimate good of international communication and cooperation.

We can take pride in the knowledge that North American casework in the 1950s, later excoriated as an obstacle to the development of social work as a force for social change, was a catalytic agent of no mean proportion in Europe. (The same claim could not be made for Asia, Africa, and Latin America.) However, in Europe casework served to renew and revitalize social work education, shattered by five years of war and isolation. It breathed new life into social work practice, replacing paternalistic approaches to people and their problems with a manner of helping that preserved human dignity. It provided the opportunity and stressed the capacity of people to grow and change and to help themselves.

Eileen Younghusband was right. But it was not a small or easy achievement for either the United States or the rest of the world to mix up Sigmund Freud with the Declaration of Independence. Things will never be the same.

REFERENCES

de Jongh, J. 1953. A European experiment in case work teaching. *Soc. Casework* 34(1):17.

———. 1951. Education for social work in Europe and its actual problems. Presented at Fifth International Conference of Schools of Social Work, Paris, 1950, p. 21.

Hurlbutt, M. E. 1920. Transplanting the American brand of social work. *The Family* 1(7):1–7.

Richmond, M. 1917. *Social Diagnosis*, New York: Russell Sage Foundation.

Smith, M. J., and E. L. Younghusband. 1953. Exporting casework to Europe. In *Education for social work*, proceedings of the First Annual Program Meeting, Council on Social Work Education, St. Louis, Mo., p. 86.

United Nations. 1958. *Training for social work: Third International Survey.* New York: Department of Economic and Social Affairs, p. 111.

Younghusband, E. 1964. Training for casework: Its place in the curriculum. In *Social work and social change. New York: Council on Social Work Education, pp. 158, 162.*

8 *Ethnic Factors and Clinical Treatment*

Frank J. Turner

Working from the assumption that ethnicity is a pervasive critical variable in all clinical practice, Turner penetrates its nature and the difficulties of precisely defining it. Misconceptions, benefits, hazards, and perplexities associated with the role ethnicity plays in our psychosocial reality are delineated. Resensitization to our own ethnic identities, as well as those of our clients, is required. Clinicians are challenged to combine the two perspectives as a resource for more effective treatment.

The relevence of the concept of ethnicity to clinical practice has long been a priority for me. It first intrigued me as a young master's graduate. In a small family agency in Canada, we became aware of an identifiable syndrome of marital problems among a large population of semirural Irish Catholics. Later, in doctoral studies, I pursued the concept of value differences between and among various ethnic groups and their effect on interview content.

Because it would be presumptuous to attempt to cover this topic in its entirety, I will consider selected components of this concept and speculate on their implications for us as clinicians. Among the many areas on which I cannot touch is a critical one, the large and grave policy issues related to this topic, issues that require societal changes to ensure that all groups have equal access to society's goods, services, and opportunities. It is not that I do not consider these changes important; they are urgent and we cannot cease our efforts to seek desired change. But this cannot be our only focus. These societal problems are not going to disappear tomorrow; our clients and their individual, group, and familial needs require services today.

I begin from the assumption that ethnicity is a critical variable in all clinical practice—one that is much more important than we have understood up to the present. It is a topic in which there is growing interest and I sense that our profession may now be at a point where we are beginning to understand its importance, subtlety, and complexity. As we struggle with this evasive concept, ideas should emerge as to directions for the further development of practice knowledge.

THE CONCEPT OF ETHNICITY

Let us begin by reviewing the concept of ethnicity, which is not as easy a task as one would first hope. One of our problems as social workers is that much of the vocabulary we use as our jargon is also used in colloquial language—for example, such words as agency, relationship, supervisor, records. This multiusage of similar words makes it difficult to keep our own concepts sharp. Ethnicity also is a word frequently used in many circles. Everyone knows what it means until we attempt to give a precise definition. Thus we all think we know what we mean by "ethnic food," "ethnic neighborhoods," and "ethnic clothes." I have even heard someone say that a certain person looked "ethnic."

Ethnicity, like the word personality, does not lend itself to a single definition even when we are trying to be precise. Clearly the term refers to particular kinds of differences between groups of people: to the concept of a collectivity, of ancestry, or of common origins; to a concept of a shared historical past, of identification with particular behaviors, beliefs, traditions, or practices; to a concept of loyalty and identification; and I suggest as well to aspirations for a common future.

Marta Sotomayor (1977) presents an excellent discussion of ethnicity in an article in *Social Casework*. She says, "Ethnicity refers to the underlying sentiment among individuals based on a sense of commonality of origins, beliefs, values, customs or practices of a specific group of peoples." For her the important aspect is a sense of historical continuity, from a highly subjective aspect. This concept of subjectivity is essential, and I shall return to it later. As with other authors, she distinquishes ethnicity from culture. Culture deals with the symbolic and universal generalities one can make about a particular group and ethnicity with the individuals' mode and depth of identification, that is, a sense of belonging to a reference group. Some of the symbolic factors on which a person's ethnic identity may be based include various combinations of physical contiguity, language or dialect, religion, physical features, kinship patterns, nationality, and history.

As with other concepts in our profession, for the present we need to be comfortable with some lack of precision. I believe it is too soon to try for a precise definition. But we do need to continue to seek that precision if we wish to expand our clinical effectiveness. There are two facets of this lack of precision that need to be mentioned. The first relates to the origin of the word ethnicity. If one goes to its Greek origins, there is unfortunately, an implied pejorative meaning. The word was first used to refer to groups who were outside of the mainstream of a society, those who were pagans or foreigners, that is, those who did not quite measure up to the self-identified reference group. This aspect—a sense of less worth, as well as a sense of minority status—is prevalent in many of our discussions about ethnicity and it becomes a confounding variable. I became interested in this implied lesser status and negative aspect of ethnicity in social work literature, and wondered if it had always been so. I reread some of the discussions about immigration in the *Proceedings* of the Annual Charities Meeting in 1884–1885, and was quite surprised to find that even 100 years ago a strong value theme existed that reflected clearly the long tradition of deserving and nondeserving clients. In 1884 there were strong comments about desirable and undesirable immigrants, comments that implied a strong sense of moral rectitude. I believe that these earlier ideas account, partially at least, for our continuing to see ethnicity in a one-down position, forgetting that we all are members of at least one ethnic group, and frequently of several.

The second difficulty in the use of terminology, is to co-identify the term ethnic with concepts of class, culture, and minority status, especially an oppressed minority. As we said earlier, ethnicity is different from culture. It is also different from socioeconomic class. Thus you can find members of many ethnic groups at all socioeconomic strata. Ethnicity is also not coterminous with race. There are many ethnic groups within various racial groups, as well as ethnic groups that cut across racial lines. There are many ethnic groups that are not oppressed minorities, just as there are many minorities who are not oppressed.

We err seriously if we continue to co-identify ethnicity with minority status, especially oppressed minority membership. Obviously as practitioners we know that each of these terms is important in practice, and each interrelates with various aspects of ethnicity, but each needs to be perceived as a separate idea to understand accurately when and how they interact.

While a dean in a Canadian school of social work that was also a member of the Council on Social Work Education (CSWE),

I became very aware of problems with this restricted use of ethnicity. Each year I would receive questionnaires asking me for the ethnic distribution of faculty and students, but that only included, if I remember correctly, the categories of black, white, Asian-American, Chicano, Puerto Rican, and Indian. Each year I would write back and describe the faculty as French-Canadian, Barbadian, American black, Irish Catholic, Ukranian, Hindu, Newfoundlander, and so on. In fact it was this co-identification with minority that was one of the critical factors in the decision of the Canadian schools of social work to withdraw from CSWE. In particular my French-Canadian collegues in Quebec objected vehemently to being referred to as a minority group, as was frequently done in discussions concerning accreditation of Canadian schools.

I believe it is counterproductive and an oversimplification to divide groups into minority and majority status. I suggest it would be more useful to view these two terms as ends of a continuum along which all groups in society can be placed, with the understanding that there is constant movement of various groups in both directions. Thus all ethnic groups range somewhere along the line of minority and majority. To use minority and not majority results in our insensitivity to the richness and pervasiveness of ethnicity and a failure to tap appropriately this influencing but nondetermining aspect of our personalities as a variable in treatment.

I want to stress the idea that ethnicity is a delicate and frequently subtle aspect of our personalities. I stress this because of our tendency to restrict many of our discussions of ethnicity to political issues, as real and critical as these are. In so doing we fail to appreciate the more complex and highly influential nuances of ethnicity present in our cases. This view of ethnicity in a gross sense is reflected in most recent social work literature. A review of it would quickly lead one to conclude there are indeed only a few discrete ethnic groups, yet we all know that in Canada and the United States they number in the hundreds. The *Harvard Dictionary of Ethnicity* lists 106 groups in the U.S., most of which would also be identifiable in Canada. In addition to the number of discrete ethnic groups, as clinicians we need to take into account the many subgroups that exist within groups. Such subgroups can have identity values, customs, histories, traditions, beliefs, and aspirations that diverge widely within the larger ethnic group. In the past couple of years, my wife Joanne, and I have been involved in a Croatian group where this factor clearly emerged. Croatia is a small country, yet the number of existing distinct subgroups is astounding. There are clear differences based not only on from which valley someone originated, but also on the side of the valley the person lived. These highly influential, although hidden, factors often have essential ramifications in many facets of a client's psychosocial reality. As clinicians we need to understand these.

We do not do this when we view ethnic identity in large sociopolitical segments. However, I believe this is changing. I believe we are becoming more aware as fellow passengers on this "Spaceship Earth" that it is possible, desirable, and necessary to build nations on the basis of recognized and supported cultural pluralism rather than assimilation. If this is true, we will be more responsive to ethnic reality.

ETHNICITY'S ROLE IN PSYCHOSOCIAL REALITY

Let us now look at the role that ethnicity plays in our psychosocial reality. Building on my earlier comments, I begin by considering ethnicity as a neutral term that can contribute to an individual, family, or group's healthy psychosocial reality or have a detrimental negative impact.

Initially I take a positive position, presuming some health and normality in the situation, and save for later some of the problematic factors that need to be considered in our assessments and diagnoses. I also take as given that we all have an ethnic identity. Let me stress this latter point so that we avoid co-identifying the concept of ethnicity and the term minority.

Certainly the first thing that our ethnic identity does for us is to give us a place in history. This is probably one of its most important contributions. With little effort of our own, our ethnic inheritance identifies us with the complex inheritance of ideas, traditions, preferences, values, perceptions, tastes, and views of reality that are a part of a particular configuration of tradition.

Our ethnicity thus gives us a vertical sense of connectedness, to use Pinderhughes' (1984) concept. It also gives us a horizontal linkage to others who function and perceive the world in the same way. Thus it can give us a sense of place and worth and protect us from being cut off from the past and abandoned in the present. In the present our ethnic identity can serve to link the individual and familty to larger bureaucratic groups. This intermediary function may be becoming more and more important in one mass pluralistic society by providing a manageable reference group.

Essentially this can be seen as a positive but, as we know from practice, strong identifications can also function as restrictions that limit one's range of potential. The bases on which we become bound to a particular ethnic group vary from situation to situation, and include such things as language, history, religion, color, and place of origin. Language is a powerful form of indentification, and as practitioners we know how subtle can be the various levels of communication even when persons are theoretically speaking the same language. In practice even as simple a thing as how people address each other can be highly significant and sensitive.

This tradition that connects us to history affects the way we see ourselves in relation to the rest of the world: it affects the way we see the world, the things we value, the nature and pattern of our relationships, the scope and nature of our ambitions, our belief system; our perception of our abilities, and the kinds of problems that we will attempt to solve as well as the permissible range of methods we will use to solve such problems. It affects how we speak and how we behave in many critical life situations, such as birth, death, illness, and marriage. In sum our ethnic identity becomes a powerful filtering system for the processing of the daily mass of information to which our senses differentially respond.

Note that I am using the verb affect, rather than determine, to make the point that powerful as our ethnic identity can be, it does not necessarily lock us immutably into some type of destiny. Rather it equips us, or infects us, depending on how you view it, with a way of understanding who we are in terms of our evolutionary origins as we find our way through the myriads of generations that put us on the world scene at this particular moment in history. Obviously much of what we say about our ethnic identities is similar to what we would say about our family of origin, but in a much broader context, for our ethnic identity connects us not only to a particular family, but also to a larger cluster of people that may well number in the millions.

This concept of a group identity is important because of the secondary role of our ethnic identities. Thus not only does our ethnic identity give us a complex set of responses to help us put some meaning to our experiences and equip us to sort out much of what surrounds us, but it also greatly influences the way that much of our significant environment perceives us and responds to us. Obviously an aspect of the wider social systems' response to our ethnic identity is related to how evident this identity is to those with whom we come into contact and to when it becomes evident.

We have all had experiences in which the dimensions of a social situation have changed when we identified ourselves from the perspective of our ethnic identity, for example; "By the way, do you know that I am a Catholic or (or French-Canadian, and so on)?" It is important to note that such responses are not always negative. It may well be that our being identified as a member of some component of an ethnic group brings with it a whole range of positive benefits and entrée into a supporting social system.

One apsect of how we see others, and how we are perceived by others, is that almost all types of comparisons become hierarchically oriented. It is difficult to accept differences and not, at the same time, to say one is better than the other. The height of maturity is to be comfortable with one's identity and to recognize, accept, and value differences in others. So often, though, our ethnic identity is built on the basis that "those others," sometimes specific, sometimes generalized, are less good because they are not us. Identity is maintained by fostering a presumed conflict.

When people are uncomfortable about their ethnic identity, they often become negatively sensitive to intraethnic factors and are more critical and demanding of the other group members than are those who are not so identified.

Closely related to this "how the world sees us" component of our ethnicity is the term we in social work all understand well, stereotyping. Although the concept of stereotyping usually has a highly negative connotation, it can also be a source of positive reenforcement to someone who by virtue of being identified with some particular ethnic group, is endowed with qualities the person may not actually possess. I have been interested in this positive aspect of stereotyping since coming to New York from Canada and having people frequently say to me, "You Canadians are all friendly." Let me assure you that some of the least friendly people I know are Canadians. Since the concept of stereotyping is inherently a pejorative, we need to find an acceptable concept to use to identify those generalizations that we make about a group, with the understanding that they do not apply to everyone. One that I like is that of "central tendencies," used by James W. Leigh (1985).

There is a third component of personality that results from the interaction of these two important functions of ethnicity. Since our ethnic identity influences the way the world differentially sees us, depending on the ethnic identity of the viewer, our own ethnic identity often conditions us to expect particular kinds of behavior in particular situations. That is, our ethnic identity not only influences how we see ourselves in relation to others, but also creates an expectation of how others are going to, and do, see us and what they expect from us. Sometimes these expectations are clear and well defined, and sometimes they are diffuse or unknown. This in turn can create uncertainty and challenge or restrictive anxiety.

ETHNICITY AND CLINICAL PRACTICE

Let us consider some components of clinical practice and speculate on some of the ramifications of ethnicity. I think much of what I am going to say we know, but as yet we are not making use of it. Over and over again, I see records, or I am in consultation or discussion about a client, and find no information about the client's ethnicity and its strength or stress in his or her life.

Assessment and Diagnosis

My principal thesis is that in much of current practice we underattend the importance of ethnicity in assessment and diagnosis. I have already alluded to the fact that we need to be aware of the broad diversity of ethnic groups and to avoid being conditioned to think only of the seven or eight most discussed. At the same time, we need to recall that there are hundreds of various combinations of ethnic groups through marriage and other historical events. This results in probably thousands of possible combinations. I emphasize this to urge us to bring subtlety to our diagnoses and to appreciate that this aspect of a client's reality needs to be looked at carefully and skilfully in each situation. I suggest we have been so overwhelmed by the enormity of the problems related to racial issues that we have neglected to give sufficient attention to ethnicity's operation and significance in individual cases. Giordano and Levine (1985) have spoken of the increasing number of marriages across ethnic lines, and suggest this will increase even more. If so, then the assessment of a client's ethnic identity will become more complex and necessarily individualized.

There are many things we want to know about this aspect of our client. Obviously how and when we will gather this information will depend on our assessment of priorities and perception of timing in any individual case. First we want to know the client's ethnic identity. This is rarely easily answered, even when the answer appears evident. It is so easy to err if we base decisions on such things as appearance, name, language, or stated religion. As we become more interested in this, we begin to appreciate how idiosyncratic one's ethnic identity becomes. I once conducted a research project in Toronto where there is a very large Italian community. I was looking for a small sample of Italian Catholic families and used as a definition of being Italian that all four grandparents were Italian. In using this definition I proved that there were no Italians in Toronto.

In subsequent research I have used, and continue to use, self-definition as the criterion. That is, I accept someone as Italian who claims to be so. From a clinician's perspective, this is a useful way to identify a client. When one does this, there are often interesting results. Persons whom you might not at first consider as belonging to a particular group perceive themselves as being members. The reverse also holds true, and this is important.

Further use of this concept of self-definition results in interesting differential responses within families. The reality of families with mixed ethnic origins is probably more the rule than the exception in both the United States and Canada. Thus within families children often identify with different aspects of their ethnic origins. There is some indication that this differential identification is related to who identifies with which parent, as well as to birth order and perceived roles of parents.

As clinicians it is our client's perception or identification of their origins that we want. This may well be different from an ethnic identity that society may attribute to them. Thus a Jewish woman who marries a French-Canadian may be seen, identified, and responded to as a French-Canadian, even though her own identity and the family life-style may be Jewish.

Not only do we need to know a client's identity as self-defined, but we also need to know two additional factors. The first is how clear this identity is to the person, and secondly, how strong or important it is. Obviously we observe various combinations of both strength and limitations among persons. Thus a person can claim to be Ukranian with little understanding of what this means or how it does or does not influence the person's perception and behavior.

As a part of our assessment, therefore, we want to know how much clients know, (or care) about their ethnic identity and its impact on them. Some will identify with a particular ethnic cluster with little awareness of its implications, and others may be very clear about their values, preferences, beliefs, tastes, and perceptions and not be at all aware that these are reflections of their ethnic origins. A question to keep open is whether one can have no ethnic identity from the perspective of self-definition.

As a part of wanting to know the strength and clarity of a client's ethnic identity, we want to know as well something of the client's comfort, or lack thereof, with this component of the psychosocial reality. Frequently our ethnic identity is marked by ambivalence. We can see this ambivalence in ourselves. Even though we may be essentially comfortable with our ethnic identity, we know that some aspects of it can make us feel uncomfortable, embarrassed, or at times angry. Usually those areas of discomfort are related to some stereotypic quality of our group that we recognize as having some basis. Comedians, have played on this discomfort for years.

But although much of this discomfort about ethnic identity may be strongly suppressed, it may still be playing an influential role in a client's life. General knowledge about what some authors call psychoprofiles or central tendencies of various ethnic groups can be helpful in alerting us to possible problem areas; however, these profiles are not universal and their applicability needs to be tested in particular instances.

In general we are trying to get a clear picture as to how and where a client's ethnic identity is a life positive or negative. Obviously it is rarely an either/or situation, but a mixture, and we need to specify. This is complex. It requires knowledge of clients' own perceptions of themselves as well as of society's response to their perceived ethnic group.

This raises several related questions. First, how does the client's identified ethnic group perceive itself in relation to (1) some other ethnic groups and (2) society at large? Here we get into the very negative question of ethnocentricity; that is, that form of ethnochauvinism in which a person's identity or sense of power and security is based on a perceived superiority over other groups. These perceptions of superiority are highly complex yet powerful factors in personality, and are often strongly influencing, yet unrecognized, factors in relationships between individuals, such as in marriage. I am convinced we have underestimated the extent to which such factors operate in many relationships in which we become involved. We know that in our day-to-day interaction with people such things as what part of a country one comes from, what city, what part of a city, what neighborhood, or even what street can affect the way one perceives oneself, the way one sees others, and the way one is seen by others. This type of ethnocentricity operates just as strongly within ethnic groups as between. In fact it can be extremely negative within groups. We err seriously when we attribute some interpersonal differences to intrapsychic causes, failing to recognize that they may originate from differing valuing of groups with which a person interacts. Shirley Jenkins (1981) refers to the importance of this in adoption placements of American Indian children with American Indian families, without taking into account the possibility that old tribal rivalries can make some placements acceptable and others not.

Important as it is to understand these large intergroup phenomena, as clinicians our direct interest is to understand the importance of these factors for our individual groups and families of clients. Are the clients aware of these intergroup perceptions, and how and when are they operating in a particular psychosocial profile? How much do our clients' value perceptions, patterned emotional response vocabularies, role perceptions, role expectations, beliefs, food, traditions, and customs contribute to a positive or negative self-image? How do they bring security and comfort in a situation? And how do these factors create stresses or strains in other situations?

One further aspect of the client's ethnic reality we need to consider is the way a client may use ethnicity as a defense, such as a rationalization of some aspect of functioning. I have heard clients say such things as, "I'm Irish, what can you expect?" "We Italians never do such and such," "Indians have a different time perspective, so don't expect me to keep appointments." It is comfortable to be able to blame problems, behaviors, or difficulties on one's origins and thus not have to take responsibility for them.

An important subcomponent of the diagnostic phase is the matter of perception of problems, their causes, and what is appropriate activity to cope with them. This is an area where I believe clinicians have many blind spots. I am quite sure that we have frequently assessed resistance, noninvolvement, disinterest, and lack of motivation in situations where the reality was a different perception about the cause and accepted response to identified situations.

Our overall diagnostic exercise is to assess if and where ethnic factors are operating in a case and when they need to be taken into account. Two extremes to be avoided (the first more relevant to current practice reality than the latter) are to risk minimizing ethnic factors in diagnosis, and to overemphasize so that these factors become the essence of all cases. While we are a long way from this, we know that social work has frequently manifested the pendulum phenomenon and could do so again.

Intervention

My first point here is the sensitive one of self-awareness. It is sensitive because we have all struggled, through our years of training and beyond, and often with the aid of personal therapy, to ensure that we know ourselves sufficiently well that we do not unknowingly let aspects of our personality influence the therapeutic relationship. We have done well in this area. Where I believe we have been deficient is in our failure to appreciate that other layer of personality—our ethnic identity. I have seen too many examples of case records or case presentations of experienced practitioners in which ethnic factors have been missed, where diagnostic formulations have been developed about symptoms or problems, or proposed client solutions, which could be explained as normal, appropriate, and growth-enhancing behavior from the perspective of ethnic identity. A dramatic example of this was a young native American girl who was diagnosed as schizophrenic and institutionalized on the basis of the diagnosis because she told the interviewer that she talked every night with her recently dead mother. The worker concluded that this was hallucinatory, failing to take into account that for this particular group of Indians dreams were considered a form of reality and a way of maintaining contact with the dead. Dreaming of her mother was the same as talking to her and was a healthy part of the grieving process.

We need to be ultrasensitive to ethnic factors in others. We do so where there are obvious differences between us and the client, but we still minimize the extent our own ethnic colored glasses influence values about the people with whom we come into contact. Shirley Jenkins (1981) says that we seem to accept that ethnic differences exist but then ignore their consequences in practice.

Undoubtedly we reluctantly admit to, and hence control, the large areas of bias in ourselves. What we fail to do is to recognize the more subtle ways in which we value or devalue others or their views of the world because of some component of their ethnic makeup. Just ask yourself how your perception of others is influenced by such things as an accent. This not always in a negative direction. Some accents confer status, and others do not.

Clearly some of our ethnic-based values lead us to prefer some forms of behavior in others, some theoretical models of intervention, some methods or techniques of practice. I do not suggest that everything we believe or know about intervention or appropriate behavior is based on ethnic perception. There are legitimate standards by which to assess the health or nonhealth of a situation, the appropriateness or nonappropriateness of certain behaviors, the usefulness or nonusefulness of certain models and techniques of intervention. What we have missed is the ease and frequency with which we value some behaviors and perceptions over others on professional grounds when they are normal and healthy manifestations of difference. The areas in which I believe we are most vulnerable are related to those aspects of our own ethnicity with which we are uncomfortable. I have been reinforced in these ideas by some of the material that is being reported in groups made up of practitioners who are looking experientially at their own ethnicity.

This need for self-awareness has important implications in establishing and maintaining relationships with clients. On a pragmatic level, it is important to try to understand quickly the possibility that the client's perception of us may be influenced considerably by ethnic factors. Thus regardless of our efforts to be our ourselves, we may be seen by the client variously as oracles, as confessors, as wise adults, as advisors, as tribal, clan or group elders, as healers, as advice givers, as neutral sounding boards, as evil authorities, as trusted friends, and so on. Many of these perceptions will stem from deep-rooted historical values and perceptions about the role of professional helpers.

Too often we have not appreciated that some of the actions, mannerisms, and interviewing styles we consider sustaining and assuring are perceived as anxiety producing, intrusive, and even boorish by some clients. To some, the use of first names, for example, might be unacceptable. Each of us has a set of rules that govern our behavior about things to which we subscribe carefully although rarely consciously.

I suggest that we need to continue to reflect on the concept of transference as we seek to make our practice more ethnically sensitive. I am certain that at times we have viewed some aspects of relationships as transference that could be explained better as ethnically conditioned responses to perceptions of appropriate role behavior in helping situations. I suspect, but am less certain about it, that the reverse is also true, that we miss some transference factors in particular situations for the same reason.

We are all aware of how complex the factor of the empowerment is in the helping relationship and how clients can feel themselves to be in a down position by virtue of having a problem and seeking help, which may exacerbate their feelings of powerlessness in their total life situation. As we become more ethnically sensitive, we develop a richer perspective on the power aspects of our relationships with clients. This aspect of authority in a relationship is, of course, not always a negative, but it is important that we understand its strength, structure, and parameters before we can use it effectively as a part of a helping process. We know that at times clients will endow us with power and importance that will permit them to look at themselves in a way they never would in other situations. We need to explore this further. However, if we always view these factors as undesirable transference or inappropriate reality testing, or always seek to deauthoritize a relationship, we may be doing our clients a great disservice.

In a similar way, we need to be very careful about what we consider to be appropriate manifestations of emotion, family roles, sexual activity, openness, privacy, and methods of dealing with significant life events. Those who work in the health field are well aware of the complex range of emotional and behavioral responses different groups have to illness and death. Some of these responses are highly uncomfortable for us, even though healthy and appropriate for the clients and their families.

The Intervention Process

Certainly the setting of objectives in our cases will frequently be influenced by ethnic factors. If so, we need to be careful that our own values do not impede the setting of appropriate goals with the client. If we are future oriented, we will probably favor future-oriented goals that seek to equip the client better for future life experiences. But if our client is primarily present oriented, then dealing with here-and-now tasks may be the critical reality, letting the future take care of itself.

Evidently the ethnic-sensitive clinician will have to decide in each case the weight and significance of ethnic factors. To do this requires that we need to know about that aspect of a client's life. How do we learn this? The current authorities in the field are unanimous in their contention that our most important resource is the client. This seems obvious, but I am convinced we do not sufficiently encourage or permit our clients to talk enough about this critical aspect of their lives. Again I base this viewpoint on the absence of this kind of material in cases. Even when reference is there, it is often little more than a statement that this is, for example, a Puerto Rican family.

I believe there are two factors operating here; one is a presumption that we are sufficiently ethnic responsive that we do not have to give it any more attention, and the other is that we do not know what to do with it. James Leigh (1985) stresses in his teaching that ethnic interviewing can, and frequently does, tap some very primitive feelings, and can be so intense as to be quite frightening to the practitioner, as well as to the client. Often it will touch material that clients have not admitted to themselves, and certainly not to others.

Leigh also suggests that we may be reluctant to move into this area because it tends to shift our autonomy in the interview. If we ask the client, as we must, to teach us what it means, for example to be a Jamaican student in an all-white Canadian school, we are admitting that we don't know and have to learn. He suggests that this giving of responsibility to the client helps to empower the client to take charge of his or her own life.

As we become more skillful and comfortable in drawing the client out, there is a twofold benefit. For clients it can be a growth-enhancing experience, expecially if we are able to help them positively identify with this important aspect of their lives. It also helps us to understand better areas of client strength on which we can build, as well as areas of stress, confusion, and uncertainty with which we can help. Frequently clients lack knowledge about their ethnic origins, are confused, have incorrect and distorted information and attitudes, and have identified only with the negative components of their ethnicity. The direct addressing of this material in an understanding supportive way can have dramatic effects on a client's sense of self and sense of others. As a general treatment goal, we are trying to detoxify negative stereotypes persons have about themselves and their ethnic reference group or groups. Penderhughes (1984) says, "Clinicians who are clear and positive concerning their ethnic identity are more able to help patients to be also."

I am not suggesting that this is the first thing we do in treatment, but that as we begin to appreciate the power and universality of ethnicity, we will appropriately introduce the content into our interactions with the client when and where it is needed. Obviously we cannot prescribe how best to do this in each case, although Leigh (1985) does seem to suggest it is material for early contacts. As we become more comfortable with and respectful of the differences and the nuances of the myriad ethnic factors in our lives, we can help clients recognize the role these matters play in their own lives, modify these roles if they wish, develop new respect in their own eyes, and open up the possibility of a rich cluster of strengths on which we and the clients can draw in seeking appropriate plans of intervention.

In some clearly identified ethnic situations, we all know how helpful can be the rich array of designated or targeted services, both voluntary and professional, formal and informal, that develop. But over and above clearly established ethnic services, there are a range of types of societal resources we can consider as appropriate. History, theater, literature, music, food, travel, handicrafts, folk dancing, and language training can serve to enhance identification and expand knowledge about origins and roots. We meet many persons who have so repressed or resisted some aspects of their ethnic origins and identity that they lack positive knowledge about them and can benefit greatly from their social supports.

In my list I mentioned travel. I am quite certain that we have underestimated the interesting role that access to travel has had in fostering, strengthening, and maintaining ethnic identity. In the area in which we lived last year, there was a strong working-class Italian group, and we were interested that most of the children in this group had spent several summers in Italy and were highly identified with a desire to maintain their language and ties. The same is true of the West Indians in Toronto, who frequently move back and forth between Canada and the Islands. I understand this is common with Puerto Rican families as well, and I am sure with many other groups.

Frequently the focus of our intervention is going to be directly on some aspects of the client's ethnicity. Considerable attention is currently being given to a form of therapy called ethnotherapy begun by Dr. Price Cobb, a San Francisco psychiatrist. (*St. Paul Pioneer Press*, 1983). It was first used with black clients, and subsequently with groups of Jews, Italians, and Irish through the work of Joseph Giordano and Irving Levine. In this modality groups are established that are homogeneous in ethnic makeup. They have as their focus the confronting of feelings, attitudes, and experiences about ethnic identity. The reported results have been dramatic and the group content astounding. For the first time in their lives, people confront their ethnicity in an open, emotional manner. Obviously more work needs to be done to establish useful boundaries for this treatment strategy. In addition to using this approach with clients, it has also proved useful to help groups of therapists understand their own identity better, and its role in their lives.

We need to do more work in establishing what mixes of ethnicity in groups can profit by this type of experience as well as counter indicators. Benjamin Yanoov of the University of Haifa in Israel is experimenting with groups of Israeli and Arabic young people with s similar goal. These groups have been useful in helping persons free themselves of internalized fears and stereotypes about their ethnic identity, and in particular to divest them of their magical power.

Since an important part of our ethnic identity relates to our relationship to other groups, we need to use both the strength and protection of groups to help persons learn from others and to receive support in authenticating their own ethnic group, and of equal importance, that of others, As a universe we must make huge strides in valuing differences in people, and the use of groups could be a major resource in this process.

The choice of modality in particular cases should be influenced by ethnic awareness. Since our ethnic identity affects how we view problems, and what we consider to be appropriate and desirable ways of solving them, some forms of intervention may be more acceptable and effective with some clients than others. If we remind ourselves of the Kluckholn value profiles, we know that different groups differentially value one-to-one, group, or familial relationships—yet how often do we take this factor into account in considering choice of methodology for particular clients? Frequently we use the methodology with which we are most comfortable, or the one we think is best for the client, without taking into account the client's preference. We need to pay much more attention than we have to the basis on which we decide whether to choose one-to-one, dyad, family or group intervention. One (but not the only) variable should be the client's value-based preference. In this way we need to be ready to accept that for some clients family therapy or one-to-one therapy is antithetical to their perception of appropriate and acceptable help.

Another type of intervention is joint interviewing of two clients, a methodology we use most frequently in situations where an intense two-person relationship is the focus of attention, as in marital relationships. We know that many marital difficulties hinge on such things as different role perceptions, patterns of behavior, modes of expressing feeling, importance of tradition, and appropriate sexual practice. Since many of these are directly related to our ethnic identity, I suggest that in work with couples we spend much more time in reviewing with them their ethnicity and how these factors influence their relationship. Looking at problems in this way may well diffuse some of these feelings. Dr. Judith Nelsen (in press) in her work on communication theory reminds us that even when the language is the same, nonverbal communication can vary greatly between ethnic groups. We need to disabuse ourselves and our clients of the notion that some forms of nonverbal communications are better *per se* than others. We have all seen examples of where the avoidance of eye contact was seen as disinterest, rudeness, or guilt, when in fact it was a misunderstood sign of respect. Helping couples examine these areas in their relationship, along with other intrapsychic factors, can be helpful.

The same point as was made about methodology needs to be made about the differential use of theories or thought systems. Although we have said that social work theory and intervention were built on a value base of white middle-class America, this may be a myth. It certainly is an oversimplification because it fails to take into account the wide range of different viewpoints about various aspects of intervention and considers theory and practice as if they were a monolithic structure. I have long been interested in the existence of the 20–25 major thought systems that influence current social work clinical practice, and why some practitioners are more drawn to some theories or cluster of theories than others. Clearly many factors are involved, but one to which we have not given sufficient attention is that of the ethnic identity, particularly the value orientations and perceptions of the most valued problem-solving approaches of therapists. I have recently begun to examine this question in some detail, and believe that therapists choose particular therapy systems because of a perceived goodness of fit to their own values. If this is true, we need to give more attention to the same factor in clients. I am sure there are some clients who can identify better with a Gestalt approach than with a client-centered one, who prefer psychoanalysis to life model, and on and on. If we could see these systems as neutral, to be used as appropriate, we could enrich our practice considerably. This approach would also help us identify what kinds of ethnic identity do not fit well with any of our current systems and thus lead to the development of new approaches. The current interest in empowerment as a basis of clinical practice would seem to be an example of a new approach to practice that is a response to an identified ethnic need.

THE DELIVERY OF SERVICES

I would like to touch briefly on some service-delivery issues as a part of clinical practice. The first is the question of the ethnic agency. I trust we are long past the point where we are suggesting that such agencies are redundant. They are needed in particular times in history, in particular areas, to provide specific needs in a manner acceptable to the client. But the entire helping network, as well, needs to be much more sensitive to ethnic issues. As this happens it should be reflected in our services. It will be seen in such things as visible support for difference, a respect for other languages, acknowledgment of different traditions and customs, support for value differences, and response to holidays, traditions and customs. When possible multilingual practitioners, as well as receptionists and other workers, the provision of competent translating and interpretation services, and the availability of multilanguage materials should be considered. As we learn to appreciate the number of ethnic groups and ethnic combinations that exist, we will realize that we cannot respond to every group in the same manner. Nor need we. What we can do is convey our interest in and recognition of the importance and positiveness of diversity in a general way. More specifically, much richer use could be made of available technology to help in translations, to make information available on videotapes in many languages, and to store and have rapid access to information about many different ethnic groups and subgroups met in practice.

The point about up-to-date information relates to one additional treatment consideration. We tend to view a client's, and our own, ethnic identity as a fixed aspect of personality. This is not so. Although our ethnic groups are fixed historically and maintain an identifiable existence, the system boundaries are highly permeable. Ethnic groups are living systems in the process of constant change. So, too, is their impact on us. We need to remember that our ethnic identities emerge, develop, and are modified. This is just as true of ethnic groups as it is of individuals within various groups. Many Irish Catholics, for example, are very different in values and world view today than they were a generation ago. Groups, as well as individuals, change at different rates. In treatment we do not accept that we cannot change our view of the world and how we relate to it. A conscious part of our therapy is always to help people refocus their views of themselves, their attitudes, their beliefs, their behavior, their perception of others, their goals. Understanding the strengths, dimensions, and parameters of our ethnic identity helps us to assess where change is possible, where other alternatives are acceptable, and what outcomes are permissible.

One of the implications of a renewed ethnic interest is that it pushes us back to our roots. In this regard I was interested in seeing what we said about ethnicity and was pleased to find that in 1924 the Conference on Social Work was held in Canada rather than in the United States. At that conference J. S. Woodsworth (1924), a famous Canadian socialist politician and the father of a well-known Canadian social worker/educator, said the following in a paper on immigration legislation and the goal of assimilation.

> Are we egotistical enough to really want the immigrant to be made like ourselves? Heaven forbid! We have in practice taken for granted that our standards were the only and final standards. If the immigrant has not in all points measured up to our standards, we have considered him as an inferior.
>
> Some of the immigrants have been more concerned in making homes than in making money and we have called them unambitious. Some have given considerable time to participating in musical and dramatic performances and we have called them shiftless and lazy. Some have clung to the religious beliefs of their fathers and to the associations of the homeland and we have called them superstitious and unpatriotic. Some have wished their children to retain a knowledge of their mother-tongue, and we have denounced them as reactionary and un-Canadian. In our nation building we need the wise master-builders, who understanding the value of each class of material, can fit each piece in its place in the ever-enlarging picture. (pp. 92–101)

As we carry on our practice, let us make strong efforts to resensitize ourselves to three things: (1) our own ethnic identities and their influences on our view of ourselves and others; (2) the ethnic identities of our clients; and (3) how to combine the first two into a resource to serve more effectively those clients for whom we are responsible.

REFERENCES

Ethnic therapy. 1983. *St. Paul Pioneer Press*, p. 3c.

Giordano, J., and I. Levine. 1985. A look at intermarriage in the U.S. *N. Y. Times*, Feb. 11, p. C13.

Greene, J. W., and L. Wilson. 1983. An experimental approach to cultural awareness training. *Child Welf.* 6(4):303–311.

Harvard encyclopedia of American ethnic groups. S. Thernstrom et al. (Eds.). 1980. Boston: Harvard University Press.

Jenkins, S. 1981. *The ethnic dilemma in social services.* New York: Free Press.

Katlin, F. 1982. The impact of ethnicity. *Soc. Casework* 63(3):168–171.

Leigh, J. W. 1985. Ethnic competence in social work practice: The ethnographic interview. Presented at 1985 Annual Program Meeting, Council on Social Work Education, Washington, D.C.

Nelsen, J. C. In press. Communication theory and social work. In *Social work treatment*, 3rd edition, F. J. Turner (Ed.). New York: Free Press.

Pinderhughes, E. B. 1984. Teaching empathy: ethnicity, race and power at the cross-cultural treatment interface. *Am. J. Soc. Psychiatry* 4(1):5–12.

Solomon, B. 1980. Alternative social services and the black woman. In *Social services for women.* New York: Columbia University Press, pp. 333–340.

Sotomayor, M. 1977. Language, culture and ethnicity in developing self-concept. *Soc. Casework* 58(1):195–203.

Woodsworth, J. S. 1924. Immigration legislation and its administration as it bears upon the problem of assimilation in Canada. In *Conference of Social Work, 1924.* Chicago: University of Chicago Press, pp. 92–101.

Wynetta, D., and E. Schlesinger. 1981. *Ethnic sensitive social work practice.* St. Louis: Mosby.

Yanoov, B. Personal correspondence.

Index

ABOUT THE EDITORS

Phyllis Caroff, D.S.W., is Professor in the Hunter College School of Social Work and Director of the Post Masters Program in Advanced Clinical Social Work. Dr. Caroff is also in private practice in New York City.

The late Mary Gottesfeld, M.S.S., was Adjunct Full Professor in the Hunter College School of Social Work and chaired Individual Therapy Concentration within the Post Masters Program in Advanced Clinical Social Work. In addition, Ms. Gottesfeld maintained a private practice in New York City.